# Carry Alongs

## 15 Crochet Handbags & Purses
### *for Every Occasion*

*Carrie A. Sullivan*

**kp** **krause publications**
*An Imprint of F+W Publications*

First published in North America in 2008

An Imprint of F&W Publications
700 East State Street • Iola, WI 54990-0001
715-445-2214 • 888-457-2973

and
Dimensional Illustrators, Inc.
P.O. Box 543
Southampton, PA 18966
215-953-1415

Library of Congress Control Number: 2007928270


ISBN-10: 0-89689-656-0
ISBN-13: 978-089689-656-7

Printed in China


10 9 8 7 6 5 4 3 2

*I dedicate this book to five special women in my life:*
*my grandmother, Grace; my mother, Carol; my aunt, Toni;*
*and my sisters, Colleen and Chrissy, for their artistic*
*influence, encouragement, and love throughout my life.*

## Acknowledgments

Thanks to Nick and Kathleen Greco for the faith, professional guidance, and friendship you offered throughout the writing of this book. Thanks to Deborah Davis for capturing my style with your graphic design. Marty Miller, thanks for your suggestions and help with a first-time pattern writer. Photographer Joe VanDeHatert and his wife Wendy, thank you for the most beautiful pictures and a great experience. Photos shot on location at the Nash Hotel in South Beach, Florida. Thanks to Judy Patkos for going above and beyond for me! To Ruth Kempner, owner of Knit Together, thanks for all your support. My gratitude extends to the following contributors for their support and generosity: Berroco, Inc., Bag-E-Bottoms, Boomerang Professional Crochet Hooks, Crystal Palace Yarns, Jelly Yarns®, Knit One, Crochet Too, Inc., Knitting Fever, Inc., Louisa Harding Yarns, Muench Yarns, M&J Trimming, and Plymouth Yarn Company. Thanks to all my family and friends, especially my husband, Joe, and boys, Luke and Indy, for their love and understanding throughout this new adventure; without them, I would not have been able to do it!  –Carrie

Creative Director *Kathleen Greco Dimensional Illustrators, Inc.*

Executive Editor *Nick Greco Dimensional Illustrators, Inc.*

Design and Typography *Deborah Davis Deborah Davis Design*

Crochet Designer *Carrie A. Sullivan*

Purse Lining Text *Judith Patkos and Kathleen Greco*

Schematic Illustrations *Deborah Davis Deborah Davis Design*

Fashion Photographer *Joe VanDeHatert V Studio*

Crochet Basics Photography *Kathleen Greco Dimensional Illustrators, Inc.*

Pattern Editor *Marty Miller*

Hair and Makeup Stylist *Tom Venditelli*

Purse Lining *Judith Patkos*

Evening Clutch Lining *Carol Firman*

# Table of Contents

## 2 Spring and Summer Handbags 30

**Evening Clutch 32**

**Spiral Bag 36**

**Caribbean Tote 40**

**Whimsical Bag 44**

**Drawstring Shell Carryall 48**

**Ice Princess Purse 52**

**Petals Purse 56**

# *3 Fall and Winter Handbags* 60

## *Skill Level Project Guide*

### *Beginner*

### *Easy*

### *Intermediate*

# Introduction

Handbags are important fashion accessories we love as little girls. They complete an outfit and hold our most cherished essentials. Like best friends, we take them along with us wherever we go and choose different ones throughout our life experiences. The bags in *Carry Alongs* are designed to complement the many fashion styles we encounter every day.

The wonderful collection of 15 handbags in this book features contemporary design styles and fashions from casual to dressed up for the young and the young at heart. The book features shoulder bags, clutches, and carryalls as well as drawstring and evening purses in a beautiful variety of fashion-savvy yarns. Attach an easy to crochet or ready-made handle and embellish with beads, buttons, or buckles to complete the look. Schematics help you follow and understand each design pattern. Simple instructions for lining your finished handbags are included on the pattern page. In addition, purse lining basics are discussed in the Crochet Basics chapter as a guide for professional finishing.

The handbags are designed for the fashion-conscious woman who loves the art of crochet and enjoys creating beautiful, contemporary purses that are fun to make and chic to wear. Enjoy this book as you crochet your own purses to cherish and carry along all year-round!

# 1
# Crochet Basics

This first chapter is valuable for both novice and seasoned crocheters. Full-color, step-by-step photographs guide you from an initial foundation chain through basic stitches, such as the slip stitch, single crochet, double crochet, half double crochet, long double crochet, and treble crochet. Working in the round is explained and demonstrated with creating a center ring and increasing in the round. Many special decorative stitches are used to embellish the handbag projects including the cluster stitch, Caribbean Tote; the shell stitch, Drawstring Shell Carryall and Shell Sack; the overlay chain stitch, Harlequin Barrel Bag and Striped Demi Bag; the rose and leaf designs, Grace Purse; the bullion stitch, Harlequin Barrel Bag.

The Ice Princess Purse and Beaded Evening Purse both feature beaded crocheting. Instructional photos illustrate how to crochet the beaded chain, beaded single, beaded double, and beaded scallop stitches. Learn the unique Tunisian/Afghan knit and simple stitches used to create the sturdy Messenger Bag. Finishing and assembly are demonstrated with fastening off, joining seams, and weaving in ends. A purse lining basics primer section is included for adding that finishing touch to your crochet purse. Use this chapter as a quick visual guide to crochet basics or as a friendly refresher if you're just getting back into crocheting.

## ABBREVIATIONS

| | |
|---|---|
| * | repeat instructions following single asterisk as directed |
| ** | repeat instructions between asterisks as many times as directed |
| " | inch(es) |
| approx | approximately |
| bdc | beaded double crochet |
| beg | beginning |
| bs | bullion stitch |
| bsc | beaded single crochet |
| ch(s) | chain stitch(es) |
| cl(s) | cluster stitch(es) |
| cm | centimeter(s) |
| cont | continue |
| dc | double crochet |
| dec | decrease |
| dtr | double treble |
| FPdc | front post double crochet |
| hdc | half double crochet |
| inc | increase |
| ldc | long double crochet |
| lp(s) | loops |
| m(s) | meter(s) |
| mm(s) | millimeter(s) |
| patt | pattern |
| PM | place marker |
| rnd(s) | round(s) |
| (RS) | right side |
| sc2tog | single crochet 2 together |
| sc3tog | single crochet 3 together |
| sc | single crochet |
| sc dec | single crochet decrease |
| sl st | slip stitch |
| sp(s) | space(s) |
| st(s) | stitch(es) |
| t-ch | turning chain |
| Tks | Tunisian knit stitch |
| tog | together |
| Tss | Tunisian simple stitch |
| tr | treble crochet |
| (WS) | wrong side |
| yd(s) | yard(s) |
| yo | yarn over |
| yoh | yarn over hook |

## US AND UK TERMINOLOGY

| US | UK |
|---|---|
| ch – chain | ch – chain |
| slip st – slip stitch | ss – slip stitch |
| sc – single crochet | dc – double crochet |
| dc – double crochet | tr – treble |
| hdc – half double crochet | htr – half treble |
| tr – treble | dtr – double treble |
| dtr – double treble | trtr – triple treble |
| yo – yarn over hook | yoh – yarn over hook |
| fasten off | cast off |
| skip | miss |
| gauge | tension |
| work even | work straight |

## US AND UK HOOK SIZES

| US Hook Sizes | Millimeter Sizes | UK Sizes |
|---|---|---|
| B-1 | 2.25 mm | 12 |
| C-2 | 2.75 mm | 11 |
| D-3 | 3.25 mm | 10 |
| E-4 | 3.5 mm | 9 |
| F-5 | 3.75 mm | 8 |
| G-6 | 4 mm | 7 |
| 7 | 4.5 mm | none |
| H-8 | 5 mm | 6 |
| I-9 | 5.5 mm | 5 |
| J-10 | 6 mm | 4 |
| K-10½ | 6.5 mm | 3 |
| L-11 | 8 mm | none |
| M/N-13 | 9 mm | none |
| N/P-15 | 10 mm | none |
| P/Q | 15 mm | none |
| Q | 16 mm | none |
| S | 19 mm | none |

## SLIP KNOT

To begin crocheting, you must secure the yarn on your hook by making a slip knot. Wind the yarn around in a loop, leave about 6" (15.25cm) of the tail to weave in later. Insert the hook through the loop and draw it through to form another loop. Pull gently to secure. After completing the slip knot, you will be ready to create your foundation chain.

1. Make a loop with the yarn, letting the ends hang down.

2. Draw 1 end through the loop to form another loop that you will be placing on the hook.

3. Pull gently on 1 end to secure the yarn on the hook.

## CHAIN STITCH (ch) AND FOUNDATION CHAIN

The chain stitch forms the foundation row in crochet. This stitch is similar to casting on in knitting. To begin, yarn over and the draw the yarn through the hook to form a chain. Repeat to make the foundation chain. Practice keeping the tension even and making all the chains uniform in size. When you master the chaining technique, you'll be ready to learn the basic single crochet stitch.

1. With the yarn secured on the hook, begin making the 1st chain stitch by wrapping the yarn from the back around to the front of the hook, this is called a yarn over. (yo)

2. Draw the hook through the loop to make the 1st chain.

3. Repeat step 2 by making another yo and drawing this loop through the loop on the hook. Practice making several chains until you feel comfortable with this stitch.

## SLIP STITCH (sl st)

The slip stitch is used in many ways such as, joining yarns, finishing, creating a ring or binding off. If the first stitch of a row or round is a slip stitch, you usually chain 0 or 1 at the end of the previous row or round to get to the correct height. To begin, make a number of foundation chain stitches, or work the next stitch indicated.

1. Insert the hook into the 2nd chain from the hook, or next stitch indicated.

2. Yo by wrapping the yarn around the hook from the back to the front.

3. Pull the hook through the chain or stitch.

4. Then pull through the 1st loop on the hook. (1 loop on hook)

## SINGLE CROCHET (sc)

The single crochet stitch is a basic stitch in crochet. This fundamental stitch creates a tight, densely packed fabric that is ideal for pieces that require close stitching. If the first stitch of a row or round is a single crochet, you usually chain 1 at the end of the previous row or round to get to the correct height. To begin, make a number of foundation chain stitches, or work the next stitch indicated.

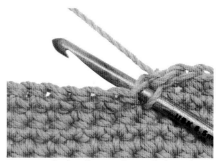

1. Insert the hook into the 2nd chain from the hook, or into the stitch indicated.

2. Yo by wrapping the yarn around the hook from the back to the front.

3. Pull up a loop through the chain or the stitch. (2 loops on hook)

4. Yo again and draw through the 2 loops. (1 loop on hook) Repeat steps 1–3 as needed.

## DOUBLE CROCHET (dc)

The double crochet stitch has three times the height of a single crochet. If the first stitch of a row or round is a double crochet, you usually chain 3 at the end of the previous row or round to get to the correct height. To begin, make a number of foundation chain stitches, or work the next stitch indicated.

1. Yo and insert the hook into the 4th chain from the hook, or the stitch indicated. The first 3 chains at the beginning count as a double crochet.

2. Yo and pull up a loop through the chain or the stitch. (3 loops on hook)

3. Yo and draw the hook through the first 2 loops. (2 loops on hook)

4. Yo and draw the hook through the remaining 2 loops. (1 loop on hook) Repeat steps 1–4 as needed.

## HALF DOUBLE CROCHET (hdc)

Half double crochet stitches are slightly less dense than single crochet stitches and half the height of double crochet stitches. If the first stitch of a row or round is a half double crochet, you usually chain 2 at the end of the previous row or round to get to the correct height. To begin, make a number of foundation chain stitches, or work the next stitch indicated.

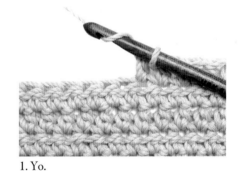

1. Yo.

2. Insert the hook into the 3rd chain from the hook, or the stitch indicated. The first 2 chains at the beginning may count as a half double crochet.

3. Yo and pull up a loop through the chain or stitch. (3 loops on hook)

4. Yo and draw through all 3 loops.

## FRONT POST DOUBLE CROCHET (FPdc)

Front post stitches are raised stitches on the right side of the fabric. Work around the post of the stitch from the previous row. Front post stitches are often used to make cable or rib stitches. The post stitch is also called a raised stitch. The Nautical Shoulder Bag features the front post double crochet.

1. Yo. Insert hook from front to back to front around post (vertical bar) of stitch indicated.

2. Yo and pull up a loop.

3. Yo and draw through 2 loops, 2 times. Repeat steps 1–3 as needed.

## LONG DOUBLE CROCHET (ldc) AND V STITCH

Long double crochet stitches are worked into the tops of stitches or the spaces between stitches one or more rows below the current row. This stitch produces a spike on both sides of the fabric. Working two long double crochet stitches in the same stitch produces a V stitch. The Satchel features the long double V stitch.

1. Yo, insert the hook in the stitch indicated 3 rounds below the round or row you are currently working.

2. Yo and pull up a loop to the height of the working row.

3. Yo and pull through 2 loops, 2 times. V Stitch: Skip stitch behind long double crochet, single crochet in next stitch, long double crochet in same stitch as the last long double crochet. V stitch is complete.

## TREBLE CROCHET (tr)

The treble crochet stitch creates longer openings between stitches and rows or rounds, resulting in a loose fabric. If the first stitch of a row or round is a treble crochet, you usually chain 4 at the end of the previous row or round to get to the correct height. To begin, make a number of foundation chain stitches, or work the next stitch indicated.

1. Yo 2 times. Insert the hook into the 5th chain from the hook, or the stitch indicated. The first 4 chains at the beginning count as 1 treble crochet.

2. Yo and pull up a loop through the chain or the stitch once. (4 loops on hook)

3. Yo and draw through 2 loops, 3 times. (1 loop on hook) Repeat steps 1–3 as needed.

## DOUBLE TREBLE CROCHET (dtr)

Taller than a treble crochet stitch, the double treble is ideal for lacy designs. If the first stitch of a row or round is a double treble crochet, you usually chain 5 at the end of the previous row or round to get to the correct height. These 5 chains count as one double treble crochet for the next row or round. To begin, make a number of foundation chain stitches, or work the next stitch indicated.

1. Yo 3 times. Insert the hook into the 6th chain from the hook, or the stitch indicated.

2. Yo and pull up a loop through the chain or the stitch once. (5 loops on hook)

3. Yo and draw through 2 loops, 4 times. (1 loop on hook) Repeat steps 1–3 as needed.

## SINGLE CROCHET 2 TOGETHER (sc2tog)

The single crochet 2 together decrease is a shaping stitch that makes a crocheted piece narrower. A single crochet is started on 2 consecutive stitches, then completed by pulling through 3 loops. It is generally worked on or near the edge of rows, or stitch markers in the round, to create gradual slanting shapes as outlined in a specific pattern.

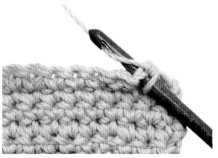

1. Insert hook into next stitch and yo.

2. Pull up 1 loop. (2 loops on hook)

3. Repeat steps 1 and 2. (3 loops on hook)

4. Yo and draw through all 3 loops. (1 loop on hook)

## SINGLE CROCHET 3 TOGETHER (sc3tog)

The single crochet 3 together decrease is a shaping stitch that makes a crocheted piece narrower. A single crochet is started on 3 consecutive stitches, then completed by pulling through 4 loops. In the Satchel pattern, the sc3tog is worked near the edge of the round, to create a tapered slanting shape.

1. Insert hook into next stitch, yo, and pull up 1 loop. (2 loops on hook)

2. Repeat step 1. (3 loops on hook)

3. Repeat step 1 again. (4 loops on hook)

4. Yo and draw through all 4 loops. (1 loop on hook)

## CREATING A CENTER RING

Creating a center ring is one way to create the foundation for all rounds in crochet. Work in the round to make seamless handbags and purse bottoms. To create a center ring, make a foundation chain and join the ends with a slip stitch to complete the ring. The type of stitch used to work in the round will determine the number of chain stitches you need for the center ring.

1. Chain desired amount of stitches.

2. Insert the hook into the 1st chain stitch.

3. Yo.

4. Draw the hook through the chain and the loop on the hook. (1 slip stitch)

## INCREASING IN THE ROUND

Rounds are increased in a variety of ways. Follow the increase instructions for each specific pattern in this book. As you increase the number of stitches, the circumference of the work will increase proportionally. In the round, always work with the (RS) of the work facing you, unless otherwise directed. The following projects are crocheted in the round:

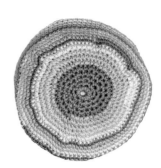

Spiral Bag: *Round Sides*

Whimsical Bag: *Oval Bottom*

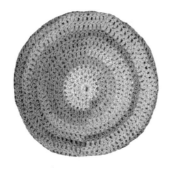

Drawstring Shell Carryall: *Round Bottom*

Petals Purse: *Oval Bottom*

## CLUSTER (cl)

The repetitive grouping of stitches, or cluster, creates a raised surface texture. To make a cluster stitch, several yarn overs are worked in the same stitch then joined together with one stitch. In the Caribbean Tote pattern, work 1 cluster in 4th chain from hook, * chain 1, skip 1 chain, work 1 cluster in next chain, repeat from * to end.

1. * Yo, then insert hook in stitch indicated, yo, pull loop through stitch.

2. Yo, pull through 2 loops. Repeat from * 4 more times in same stitch.

3. Yo, pull through first 5 loops on hook.

4. Yo, pull through last 2 loops on hook.

## SHELL PATTERN

The shell pattern in the round forms a beautiful crochet texture. To make the shell pattern, several double crochet stitches are worked in the same stitch. This stitch is worked in rounds for the Drawstring Shell Carryall in a multiple of 4 stitches plus one more stitch. Practice a row of shell stitches. Chain a multiple of 4 stitches + 1.

1. Single crochet in 1st stitch.

2. * Chain 3.

3. Work 3 double crochet in same stitch as single crochet.

4. Skip 3 stitches, 1 single crochet in next stitch. Repeat from * across.

## BULLION STITCH (bs)

The bullion stitch is created by making multiple yarn overs and pulling a loop through them. This interesting stitch creates a unique texture of coiled loops. More yarn over wraps produce a longer bullion stitch. The Harlequin Barrel Bag uses 7 yarn overs to create the bullion stitch.

1. Yo 7 times.

2. Insert the hook into the chain or stitch indicated.

3. Yo and pull up a loop.

4. Yo and draw through all the loops on the hook. 1 bullion stitch is complete. Repeat steps 1–4 as needed.

## OVERLAY CHAIN STITCH (och)

The overlay chain stitch technique creates a decorative embellishment. A chain stitch is worked along the surface of the crocheted fabric in a specific pattern. The Harlequin Barrel Bag and Striped Demi Bag feature overlay chain stitches.

1. Insert the hook from the front to the back in the stitch indicated, yo and pull up a loop (RS).

2. With (RS) facing, insert the hook in the stitch from the (RS) to the (WS).

3. Yo and pull through the stitch to make a slip stitch.

4. Repeat steps 1–3 to make overlay chain stitches as needed.

## ROSE

Crochet roses are simple to create and add a wonderful embellishment to a purse. The roses are formed by working in the round as a spiral, using half double crochet, double crochet, and treble crochet stitches in the round. The Grace Purse features crocheted roses.

1. Chain 3, slip stitch in 1st chain to form a ring.

2. Rnd 1: Chain 2 (does not count as a stitch) 8 half double crochet stitches in ring. Place marker in last half double crochet.

3. Rnd 2: In front loop only, double crochet in each of the next 8 stitches. Move marker to last stitch.

4. Rnd 3: * Treble crochet stitch in next stitch, 2 treble crochet stitches in next stitch, repeat from * to marker. Join with a slip stitch to 1st treble crochet stitch of round.

## LEAF

The leaf adds a finished element to the crocheted rose. Once the crocheted rose is complete, join a 2nd color yarn, preferably green. Crochet the leaf by working several treble crochet stitches on the outer stitches of the rose. The Grace Purse features crocheted leaves.

1. Join 2nd yarn color in any back loop of first 8 half double crochet stitches from Rnd 1.

2. Working in the back loop only, DO NOT CHAIN 4, 2 treble crochet stitches in the next stitch.

3. Work 2 treble crochet stitches in the next stitch.

4. Fasten off.

## TUNISIAN SIMPLE STITCH (Tss)

The Tunisian Simple Stitch or Basic Afghan Stitch creates a sturdy mesh fabric. The same row is worked for the forward and the return. This stitch is the basic crochet stitch used for Tunisian crochet patterns. It is used to crochet the flap of the Messenger Bag. To begin, make a number of foundation chain stitches.

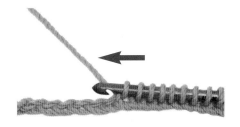

1. Row 1 (forward row): Insert hook in 2nd chain from hook, yo, pull loop through chain. Leave all loops on hook. * Insert hook into next chain, yo, pull loop through chain. Repeat from * across to end. DO NOT TURN.

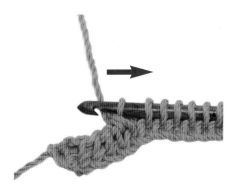

2. Row 1 (return row): Yo, pull through 1st loop. * Yo, pull through 2 loops. Repeat from * until 1 loop remains. DO NOT TURN. *Note: Loop on hook is considered 1st stitch of the next row.*

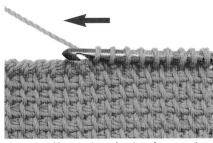

3. Row 2 (forward row): Skip first stitch. * Insert hook under single vertical bar, from right to left, yo and pull through, keep loop on hook. Repeat from * across to end. DO NOT TURN.

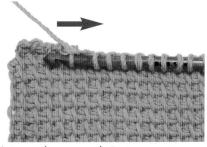

4. Row 2 (return row): Repeat step 2. Repeat steps 3–4 as needed.

## TUNISIAN KNIT STITCH (Tks)

This stitch resembles the V-shaped stockinette stitches in knitting. After completing 1 row of Tunisian Simple Stitch, the hook is inserted from front to back through the vertical bars of the chains from the previous row. The stitch is used to crochet the body of the Messenger Bag. To begin, make a number of foundation chain stitches.

1. Work 1 forward and return row of Tunisian Simple Stitch. Repeat steps 1 thru 2 above.

2. Row 2 (forward row): Skip 1st stitch. * Insert hook from front to back, between vertical bars and through next stitch, yo, pull through stitch. Leave all loops on hook. Repeat from * across, working under 2 loops on the last stitch.

3. Row 2 (return row): Yo, pull through 1st loop. * Yo, pull through 2 loops.

4. Repeat from * until 1 loop remains. Repeat steps 2–4 as needed.

## BEADED CHAIN

Beads add sparkle, shine, and glitter to any crocheted bag. This beaded chain stitch is a simple way to learn how to work with beads in crocheting. String all the beads, required in the pattern, on the yarn before starting. The beaded chain is featured on the Beaded Evening Purse.

1. Slip the bead close to the hook.

2. Yo.

3. Pull through the loop on the hook. Repeat steps 1–3 as needed.

## BEADED SINGLE CROCHET (bsc)

Before you embellish any bag with beads, make certain that the beads you have selected are the proper size and shape to fit through the yarn. String all the beads, required in the pattern, on the yarn before starting. Beaded single crochet is featured on the Ice Princess Purse pattern.

1. (RS) Slip the bead close to the hook and insert the hook into the stitch indicated.

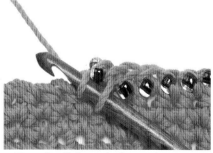

2. Yo and pull through the stitch.

3. Yo and pull through 2 loops. Push the beads through to the (RS). Repeat steps 1–3 as needed.

## BEADED DOUBLE CROCHET (bdc)

The beaded double crochet is an easy decorative way to embellish your purses. String all the beads, required in the pattern, on the yarn before starting. The beaded double crochet is formed by placing a bead in position before working each double crochet. This easy stitch is featured on the Beaded Evening Purse.

1. Slip the bead close to the hook. Yo and insert the hook into the stitch indicated. Yo and pull through the stitch.

2. Yo and pull through 2 loops.

3. Yo, and pull through the last loops. Beads will be on the (RS). Repeat steps 1–3 as needed.

## BEADED SCALLOP

The beaded scallop is an easy decorative stitch that works great for embellished edging. String beads on the yarn before beginning the pattern. The beaded scallop is formed by working several double crochets and a few beaded chains in the same stitch. This easy beaded stitch pattern is featured on the Beaded Evening Purse.

1. (WS) Work 1 double crochet, beaded chain 1, 1 double crochet, chain 1.

2. Then, 1 double crochet, beaded chain 1, 1 double crochet in 6th ch from hook or stitch indicated.

3. * Skip 3 ch. Work next beaded scallop in next ch. Repeat from * across.

## JOINING YARNS

As you follow a crocheting pattern, you will run out of yarn, want to switch yarns, or change colors. The best time to change yarns is at the end of a row. This will eliminate lumps, bumps, and knots in your finished purse. To change yarns, you work your stitch until the last yarn over. Then you work the yarn over with the new yarn.

1. Pull up a loop in the next stitch and position new yarn on the hook.

2. Draw new yarn through the last loops on the hook.

3. To work in both loose ends, insert hook in the next stitch and allow tails to remain above the hook on the tops of the stitches of the previous row or round. Work your new stitches over the tails.

## FASTENING OFF

After each section of your project is completed you will need to secure and cut the end of the yarn. This is called fastening off. Cut the yarn from the ball leaving approximately a 6" (15.25cm) tail. For higher stitches such as double or trebles leave longer tails for weaving. With the hook in the last loop, yarn over, and pull through the loop.

1. Begin fastening off by cutting a 6" (15.25cm) or longer tail from the completed project.

2. With the tail, yo.

3. Draw the tail through the last remaining loop. Pull gently to tighten.

## JOINING SEAMS

As you work with different patterns, the techniques for joining crocheted pieces will vary. The seams used to join the bags in *Carry Alongs* are not decorative, but purely functional. The flexible, nearly invisible technique we used to join seams is called the whipstitch.

1. Align edges, (WS) together, and weave yarn through several stitches to secure.

2. Insert the needle through the inside loops of the stitches to be joined.

3. Pull the needle up and over the 2 loops. Repeat steps 2 and 3 until completed.

## WEAVING ENDS

To complete your project and to prevent unraveling, you'll need to weave in the remaining tails. Work the loose ends into the crocheted fabric after your project is completed, and before it is assembled. When weaving in ends at the top of the work, work the yarn back and forth underneath the front and back loops. This technique will produce a professional-looking finish.

1. Thread the tail through a tapestry needle.

2. Insert the needle under the front and back loops of the stitch.

3. Weave the yarn back and forth under the loops of the stitches on the wrong side of the piece, if possible. Continue weaving until the yarn is completely hidden.

# Purse Lining Basics

All the patterns in this book include detailed instructions, schematics, and measurements for creating a lining to fit the finished crocheted handbags. This section offers helpful information about choosing fabrics, lining constructions, stitching, pockets, and closures. Once you have crocheted your purse, creating the lining adds durability and structure to your completed project. Creating a lining doesn't have to be a chore. The lining is a little treasure in your bag. Especially if your handbag is a gift. What a wonderful surprise for the receiver to find a bright colorful print or fingertip soft fabric on the inside!

## Fabrics for Linings

Fabrics specified for the linings are simply suggestions. To add an element of style inside your purse, choose fabrics that you prefer. Selecting a lining is part functional and part fun, and will add a professional finish to your handbag. There are various fabrics that are great for lining your purse. Cotton, cotton blends, poplin, twill, canvas, corduroy, denim, vinyl, and so forth are good lining fabrics. Be imaginative.

Use diverse prints to fit your style, such as calico, paisley, quilting prints, toile, and exotic prints. Fabric linings such as cotton or a cotton blend will work great for most handbags. If the bag is an evening or party purse, silky or soft materials such as satin polyester and faux suede (Evening Clutch, Beaded Evening Purse) would make an ideal lining. For durability, poplin is a favorite (Nautical Shoulder Bag). Choose a fabric print that is exciting, perhaps a leopard print (Messenger Bag) or pink paisley (Satchel). Whatever lining material or print you choose, be creative and have fun!

## Lining Constructions

There are a few different types of lining constructions used in this book. They are easy to create and require little hand sewing. The seams for the linings are quickly sewn by machine or can be hand sewn.

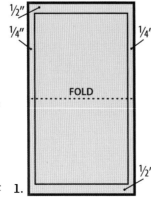

### One-Piece Folded Lining

*This lining is very simple to make. Follow the specific instructions for each pattern in this book, but here are the basic directions:*

1. Measure the height and width of your finished purse. Cut fabric

the actual width + ½" (1.25cm) for the side seam allowance, and twice the height plus 1" (2.5cm) for the top seam and fold.

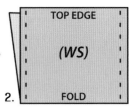

2. With (RS) facing, fold and sew together along the side seams leaving a ¼" (6mm) seam allowance.

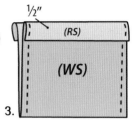

3. Fold the top edge over ½" (1.25cm) on (WS) front and (WS) back and iron. Pin the lining to the inside of the bag and hand stitch the top edge using a blind stitch.

## Cylinder Lining

*For this lining, a closed bottom cylinder shape (tube) is made. Follow the specific instructions for each pattern in this book, but here are the basic directions:*

1) For the bottom, cut fabric for the diameter of the bottom and add ½" (1.25cm). This means ¼" (6mm) around the circumference for the seam allowance. For the body, cut fabric the actual height x the circumference of the body and add 1" (2.5cm) to the width. This means ½" (1.25cm) for each side seam allowance.

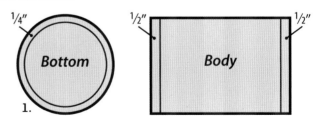

2) For the body lining, fold in half lengthwise with right sides together. Sew side seam together along the side leaving a ½" (1.25cm) seam allowance on both sides.

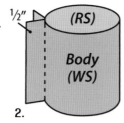

3) For the bottom circle lining, fold in half and mark the fold with pins. Fold in half in the opposite direction and mark the fold with pins. Repeat for the body. Align the bottom circle and bottom of the body edge together and pin. Sew around the seam edge of the circle bottom leaving a ¼" (6mm) seam allowance.

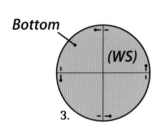

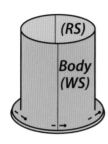

4) Fold the top edge over ½" (1.25cm) on (WS) around the circumference and iron. Pin the lining to the inside of the bag and hand stitch the top edge using a blind stitch.

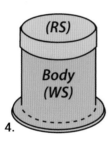

> *Drawstring Shell Carryall  48 (vertical)*
>
> *Petals Purse  56 (vertical)*
>
> *Harlequin Barrel Bag  86 (horizontal)*

## Box / Gusset Lining

*For the box / gusset lining front, back, sides, and bottom, the fabric shapes are cut, then sewn together to form a box. Follow the specific instructions for each pattern in this book, but here are the basic directions:*

1) Measure the width, height, and depth of finished purse. Cut fabric for the front, back, and sides the actual width + ½" (1.25cm) for the side seam allowance, and the actual height + ¼" (6mm) for the bottom seam and 1" (2.5cm) for the top-fold. Cut 1 piece of fabric for the bottom the actual width and height + ½" (1.25cm) for the side seam allowance.

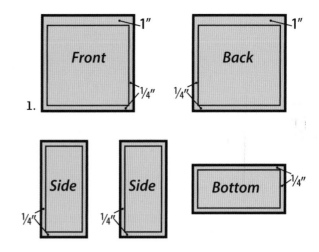

2) With the (RS) of the fabric together, sew the front and left sides of the lining together with a ¼" (6mm) seam. With the (RS) together, sew together the back and right side of the liner with a ¼" (6mm) seam.

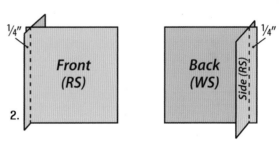

3) Sew these 2 liner units together with a ¼" (6mm) seam to form a fabric tube. With the (RS) of the bottom and the tube together, pin the bottom of the liner to the tube and sew to the base of the fabric tube with a ¼" (6mm) seam all around. Back stitch to lock in corners. Fold the top edge over ½" (1.25cm) on (WS) front and (WS) back and iron. Pin the lining to the inside of the bag and hand stitch the top edge of the liner to the bag using a blind stitch.

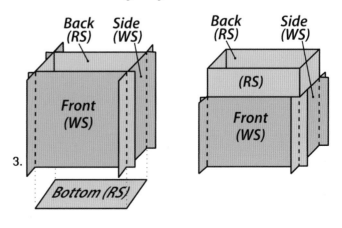

> *Nautical Shoulder Bag  66*
>
> *Grace Purse  70*

## Circular Lining with Zipper

*Follow the specific instructions for each pattern in this book, but here are the basic directions for making a circular lining with a zipper:*

1) Measure the diameter of the finished purse. Cut fabric the same diameter + 1" (2.5cm) for gusset and + ½" (1.25cm) for seam allowance. This means ¾" (2cm) all around the circumference for seam allowance. Cut 2 circles. Place circles with right sides facing together.

2) Pin the zipper or Velcro® strip to the (WS) fabric of both circles. Pin the circles together.

3) Sew circles together leaving ¼" (6mm) seam allowance. Insert the lining into the bag unzipped or unfastened. Turn the bag inside out so that the (RS) of the lining is on the outside. Pin the lining to the bag, and line up the opening of the lining to the opening of the bag. Hand stitch the lining to the bag using a blind stitch. Turn the bag right-side out.

### Stitches for Linings

The handbag linings can be machine stitched and/or hand sewn. We recommend machine stitching the side seams and hand stitching the lining to the inside of the crochet fabric. Pin the lining in place before hand sewing it in the purse.

### Blind Stitch

The blind stitch is hand stitching when you don't want to see any stitches. Use this, practically invisible, stitching method to attach the top folded edges of the finished lining to your crocheted handbag. It is also used to finish a hem or a seam by hand. Here's how:

Thread a needle with matching thread and make a knot at the end. Pass the needle under the corner and through the crease fold where you want to begin. Make sure the knot is hidden.

Slide the needle under the fabric and make three or four hidden stitches in a row (running stitches) under the fold and through the crochet fabric.

Bring the needle out through the folded edge and repeat along the edge until the seams are closed.

### Purse Support

Most fabric linings give your handbags support. However, for some designs you will need support inside the lining for added structure. Plastic needlepoint canvas was used for the Evening Clutch, Nautical Shoulder Bag, and Harlequin Barrel Bag. Use any mesh size. Trim with scissors to the measurements specified in the pattern. This is a quick, easy, and economical way to create an interior support shape.

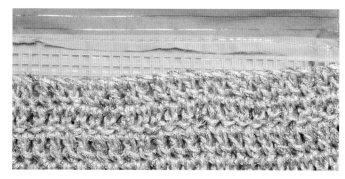

*Evening Clutch Front Support Lining  35*

*Nautical Shoulder Bag Box Support Lining  69*

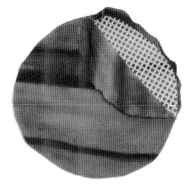

*Harlequin Barrel Bag Side Support Lining  89*

## The Pocket

*Do you need a pocket? Not really, but it makes your bag more practical. Creating a simple side pocket adds a versatile feature to your completed project. Specific instructions are included with each purse that has a pocket. Here are general instructions for making a pocket on the lining:*

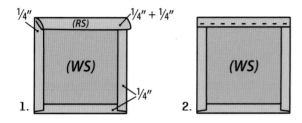

1. For the pocket, cut fabric as specified in the pattern. For the side and bottom edges, with (WS) facing, fold over ¼" (6mm) and iron. For top edge, with (WS) facing, fold over ¼" (6mm) and iron. Then, fold over ¼" (6mm) and iron again.

2. (WS) Hand stitch the top edge with a blind stitch.

3. With the (RS) facing, pin the pocket to the lining. Position the top of the pocket 1" (2.5cm) from the top edge of the lining and center the pocket from the sides. Hand stitch the side and bottom edges using a blind stitch.

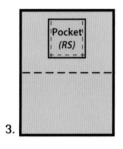

## Closures

There are several purse closures. Some handbags stay closed when the handles are held together. By using a few simple notions such as buttons, Velcro®, zippers, drawstring, or magnetic snaps, you can keep them closed for both security and a professional looking finish. Specific instructions are included with the purses that have closures.

## Magnetic Snaps

*Here are general instructions for making a magnetic snap closure:*

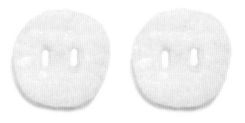

1. Mark the (WS) of the lining where the snap will be attached. Cut two circles of cardboard, needlepoint canvas or thick interfacing in a circle about ½" (1.25cm) larger in diameter than the snap. Mark the cardboard or plastic canvas where the snap prongs will go through, and cut two slits in the material.

2. Place on a larger piece of matching fabric lining and make two aligning slits through the fabric. Cover the circles with matching fabric lining. Push the snap through the fabric and cardboard, place a washer, and push the prongs down.

3. Sew assemblage to the center of the lining. Join a snap and mark a point on the opposite side of the lining.

# 2
# Spring and Summer Handbags

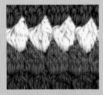
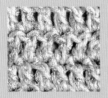

Warm weather purses are fun, easy to crochet fashion accessories. There are many handbags to fit every style and occasion. A palette of soft pastels and bright tropical colors comprise this must-have collection of purses, clutches, and pocketbooks. Seasonal fibers include colorful cotton, soft bamboo, ribbon, and vinyl yarns. Warm breezes blend perfectly with these savvy fashion accessories for casual shopping sprees, strolling along the shoreline, or chic evening wear.

Begin with simple shapes like the elegant Evening Clutch with crochet wrist strap and bamboo and metallic yarns. The Caribbean Tote is designed in tropical colors with rattan handles. For seamless finishing, try crocheting in the round. The original Whimsical Bag is designed in soft pastel cotton and ribbon yarns. Adorable and hip, the Spiral Bag is worked in two concentric single crochet circles. For an over-the-shoulder sling, the Drawstring Shell Carryall is crocheted in a beautiful shell stitch pattern. Finish with your choice of two one-of-a-kind designs. For special occasions, the vinyl Ice Princess Purse has a glossy beaded texture, while the uniquely designed Petals Purse is a guaranteed showstopper. You'll find these handbags are a sure fit for any occasion or style.

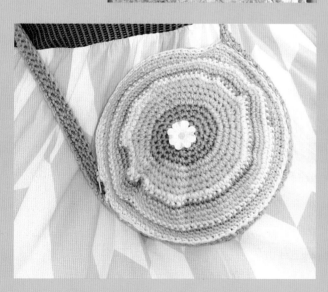

**BEGINNER**

# *Evening Clutch*

*Catch everyone's eye with this shimmering rectangular clutch accented along the flap with dangling shell buttons. Metallic and bamboo yarns create this stylish, must-have evening companion. A crocheted loop strap guarantees hands-free comfort. The alternate bag features ribbon yarn with a faux rhinestone button. Make these bags a great addition to your fashion wardrobe!*

HANDLES *Crochet*

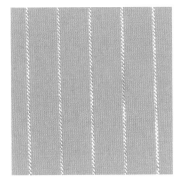

FABRIC LINING *Polyester*

EMBELLISH
*Dangling Shell Buttons*

### Yarns
A: 2 balls Plymouth Yarn *Royal Bamboo* 93yds (85m) / 50g (100% bamboo)
Color: 23

B: 1 ball Trendsetter *Jester* 110yds (101m) / 25g (80% viscose, 20% polyester)
Color: 21

### Yarn Rhinestone Alternate
C: 2 balls Louisa Harding *Glisten* 93yds (85m) / 50g (97% nylon, 3% polyester)
Color: 07

### Crochet Hook
US H/8 (5mm) crochet hook, or size needed to obtain gauge.

### Finishing Materials
40 – Dangling shell buttons (Dritz)

11" (28cm) x 4" (10cm) Plastic needlepoint canvas (any mesh)

Small sewing needle

Sewing thread

Yarn needle

Lining: polyester fabric 11½" (29cm) wide x 12½" (31.75cm) high

### Finishing Materials Rhinestone Alternate
1 – Rhinestone button

11" (28cm) x 4" (10cm) Plastic needlepoint canvas (any mesh)

Small sewing needle

Sewing thread

Yarn needle

Lining: polyester fabric 11½" (29cm) wide x 12½" (31.75cm) high

### Finished Measurements Both Clutches
Approx 11" (28cm) wide x 4" (10cm) high

### Gauge
15 sts and 8 rows = 4" (10cm) in dc with 2 strands of A and B held tog.

## Substitution Yarns

A: 2 balls Four Seasons *Classic Elite* 103yds (94m) / 50g (70% cotton, 30% wool) Color: 7697

B: 1 ball Knit One, Crochet Too *18 Karat* 224yds (205m) / 25g (65% viscose, 35% metalized polyester) Color: 120

## Substitution Yarn Rhinestone Alternate

C: 1 ball Karabella *Diamante* 92yds (84m) / 50g (70% rayon, 20% polyester, 10% nylon) Color: 14

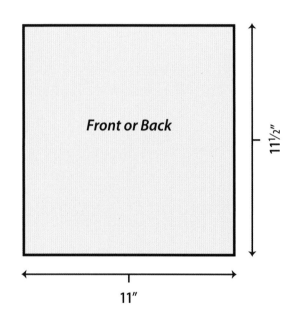

**Front or Back**

11½"

11"

# Evening Clutch Pattern

## Front or Back

With A and B held tog, ch 42.

Row 1: (RS) Dc in the 4th ch from the hook. Dc in each ch across. Turn. (40 dc, including ch-3 at beg)

Rows 2–23: Ch 3 (counts as dc here and throughout), skip the 1st st, work 1 dc in each st across. Turn. (40 dc)

At the end of Row 23, fasten off.

## Wrist Strap

With A and B held tog, ch 35. Turn, sl st in each ch across. Fasten off. Weave in all ends.

## Finishing

With the 1st row on the bottom and the (RS) facing, fold up 8 rows so that the (RS) are tog. Sew the sides tog with the yarn and yarn needle. Turn the clutch (RS) out, and fold over the flap. With the (RS) facing, attach the dangling shell button with a sewing needle and thread. Place 1 shell button at every dc of the last row. With yarn and yarn needle, attach the wrist strap to the top inside corner. Sew the 2 ends to form a loop.

## *Evening Clutch Rhinestone Alternate Pattern*

### Front or Back

With C, ch 37.

Row 1: (RS) Dc in the 4th ch from the hook, dc in each ch across. Turn. (35 dc, including ch-3 at beg)

Rows 2–23: Ch 3 (counts as dc here and throughout), skip the 1st st, work 1 dc in each st across. Turn. (35 dc)

At the end of Row 23, fasten off.

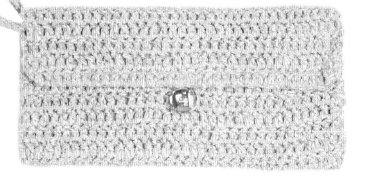

## Wrist Strap

With C, ch 35. Turn, sl st in each ch across. Fasten off. Weave in all ends.

## Finishing

With the 1st row on the bottom and the (RS) facing, fold up 8 rows so that the (RS) are tog. Sew the sides tog with the yarn and yarn needle. Turn the clutch (RS) out, and fold over the flap. Fold a 2" (5cm) piece of ribbon yarn in half to create a lp. Sew lp centered on (WS) of flap edge. Attach a button with a sewing needle and thread to the center of the front. Sew the 2 ends of the wrist strap to form a lp. With the yarn and yarn needle, attach the wrist strap to the top inside corner.

## One-Piece Folded Lining Both Clutches

*(see purse lining basics p. 26)*

Measure the width and height of either finished purse. If your purse is the same size as the given finished measurements, trim plastic needlepoint canvas: 11" (28cm) wide x 4" (10cm) high. Sew to the (WS) of the crocheted fabric, 4" (10cm) from the bottom edge.

Cut fabric the actual width + ½" (1.25cm) for seam allowance, and the actual height, including the flap, + 1" (2.5cm) for top seam and fold. If your purse is the same size as the given finished measurements, trim should measure:

11" (28cm) wide + ½" (1.25cm) = 11½" wide (29.25cm)

11½" (29.25cm) high + 1" (2.5cm)= 12½" (31.75cm) high

For the lining, fold 4" (10cm) lengthwise from the bottom edge (RS) tog to: 11½" (29.25cm) wide x 8½" (21.5cm) high. Sew tog along the side seams leaving a ¼" (6mm) seam allowance. For the top and bottom edges, fold over ½" (1.25cm) (WS) front and (WS) back and iron. Pin the lining to the inside of the bag and hand stitch the top edge using a blind stitch.

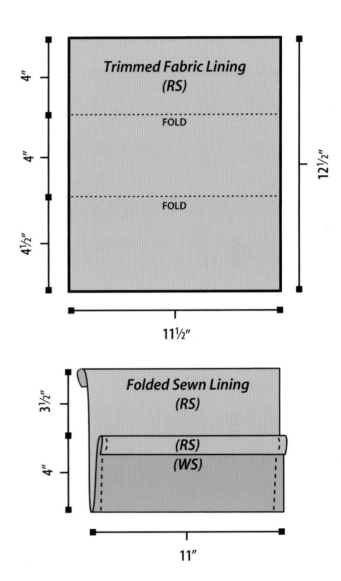

# Spiral Bag

*Round is beautiful and this cool shoulder bag is sure to turn heads. Four pastel cotton yarns are blended in the round and crocheted in a unique spiral design. This casual bag features an easy access zipper and ample gusset. Crochet a long shoulder strap for that cute, over-the-shoulder look. Add daisy buttons and voilá!*

HANDLES *Crochet*

FABRIC LINING *Cotton*

EMBELLISH *Daisy Buttons*

## Yarns

A: 1 ball Nashua *Creative Focus Cotton* 93yds (85m) / 50g (100% mercerized cotton)
Color: 15 Seafoam

B: 1 ball Nashua *Creative Focus Cotton* 93yds (85m) / 50g (100% mercerized cotton)
Color: 16 Sky Blue

C: 1 ball Nashua *Creative Focus Cotton* 93yds (85m) / 50g (100% mercerized cotton)
Color: 17 Ice Blue

D: 1 ball Nashua *Creative Focus Cotton* 93yds (85m) / 50g (100% mercerized cotton)
Color: 18 Caribbean

## Crochet Hook

US G/6 (4mm) crochet hook, or size needed to obtain gauge.

## Finishing Materials

1 – 6" (15.25cm) Zipper or Velcro® strip

2 – Daisy buttons

Needle and thread

Yarn needle

Stitch marker

Lining: cotton fabric 2 – 9½" (24cm) diameter circles

## Finished Measurements

Purse: 8" (20.25cm) x 8" (20.25cm)

Strap and Gusset: ¾" (2cm) wide x 60" (152.5cm) long

## Gauge

9 rnds and 10 sc = 2" (5cm).

*Slip Stitch (sl st)*

*Single Crochet (sc)*

## Substitution Yarns

A: 2 balls Bernat Handcrafter *Cotton Solids* 80yds (73m) / 50g (100% cotton) Color: 00001

B: 2 balls Bernat Handcrafter *Cotton Solids* 80yds (73m) / 50g (100% cotton) Color: 00088

C: 2 balls Bernat Handcrafter *Cotton Solids* 80yds (73m) / 50g (100% cotton) Color: 00083

D: 2 balls Bernat Handcrafter *Cotton Solids* 80yds (73m) / 50g (100% cotton) Color: 00010

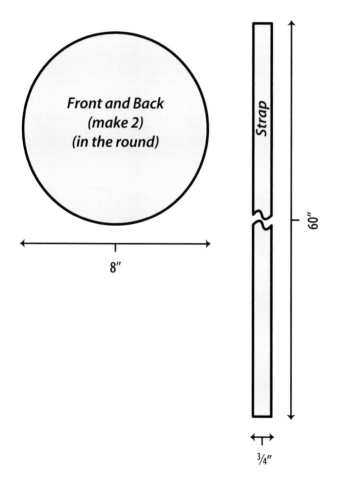

## Spiral Bag Pattern

### Front and Back (make 2)

With A, ch 4, sl st in 1st ch to form a ring.

Rnd 1: Ch 1, work 8 sc in ring, PM.

Rnd 2: Ch 1, * 1 sc in 1st sc, 2 sc in next sc, repeat from * to marker. Do not join rnd. Move marker to next rnd.

Rnds 3–5: Repeat Rnd 2. Change to B, and remove marker.

*Note: You are working in a spiral and you will need to count your sts. You do not have to mark your rnds.*

Rnd 6: Sc in each of the next 100 sc. Change to C. * Sc in next sc, 2 sc in next sc, repeat from * 19 more times, sc in each of the next 40 sc. Change to D. ** Sc in next sc, 2 sc in next sc, repeat from ** 22 more times, sc in each of the next 31 sc. *** Change to A. Sc in each of the next 100 sc. Change to B. Sc in each of the next 100 sc. Change to C. Sc in each of the next 100 sc. Change to D. Sc in each of the next 100 sc. Repeat from *** 1 more time, ending with D, sc in each of the next 200 sc.

Fasten off.

### Strap and Gusset

With A, Ch 200.

Row 1: Ch 1. Skip 1st ch. Sc in each ch to end. Ch 1, turn.

Row 2: Sc in each sc to end. Ch 1, turn.

Rows 3–4: Repeat Row 2.

Fasten off.

## Finishing

Sew the ends of the strap/gusset tog to form a circle. With matching yarn, sew 1 circle to foundation chain of the strap/gusset, centering the joined ends of the strap on the bottom, and leaving a 6" (15.25cm) opening at the top of the circle. Repeat for the other circle. Weave in all ends. Sew daisy buttons to center of circles.

## Circular Lining with Zipper *(see purse lining basics p. 26)*

Measure the diameter of the finished purse. Cut fabric the same diameter + 1" (2.5cm) for gusset and + ½" (1.25cm) for seam allowance. If your purse is the same size as given finished measurements, trim should measure:

8" (20.25cm) diameter + 1" (2.5cm) gusset + ½" (1.25cm) seam allowance = 9½" (24cm) circle.

Cut 2 – 9½" (24cm) circles. Place circles (RS) facing tog. Pin the zipper or Velcro® strip to (WS) fabric of both circles. Pin the circles tog. Sew circles tog leaving ¼" (6mm) seam allowance. Insert the lining into the bag unzipped or unfastened. Turn the bag inside out so that the (RS) of the lining is on the outside. Pin the lining to the bag, and line up the opening of the lining to the opening of the bag. Hand stitch the lining to the bag using a blind stitch. Turn the bag right-side out.

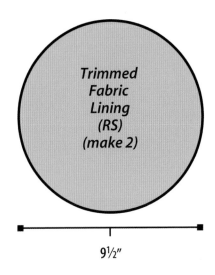

Trimmed Fabric Lining (RS) (make 2)

9½"

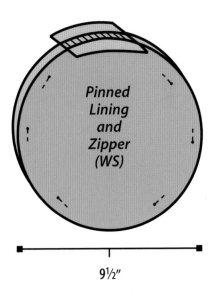

Pinned Lining and Zipper (WS)

9½"

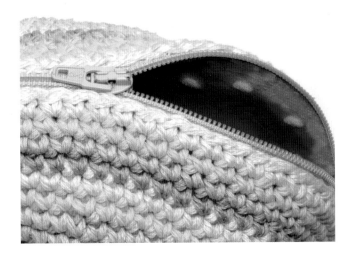

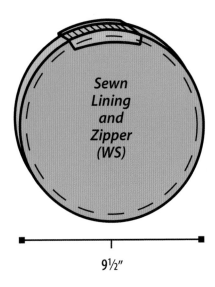

Sewn Lining and Zipper (WS)

9½"

# Caribbean Tote

*The tropical colors and A-shaped bamboo handles make this cluster-stitch tote the perfect vacation companion. Bright, colorful variegated cotton yarns accent this simple, yet stylish purse. The lined bag features a magnetic clasp for added convenience and safety. Crochet a petit, blue-green alternate for the ideal summer carry along for all the essentials.*

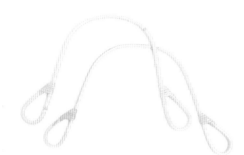

HANDLES *Rattan Loop*

PETIT ALTERNATE HANDLES *Bamboo*

FABRIC LINING *Cotton*

**Yarn**

2 balls Katia *Jamaica* 219yds (200m) / 100g (100% cotton) Color: 4009

**Yarn Petit Alternate**

2 balls Katia *Jamaica* 219yds (200m) / 100g (100% cotton) Color: 4010

**Crochet Hook**

US G/6 (4mm) crochet hook, or size needed to obtain gauge.

**Finishing Materials**

2 – Rattan loop handles

1 – ¾" (2cm) Magnetic snap

Yarn needle

Lining: cotton fabric 12½" (31.75cm) wide x 18½" (47cm) high

Pocket lining: cotton fabric 7" (17.75cm) wide x 5¾" (14.5cm) high

**Finishing Materials Petit Alternate**

2 Bamboo handles

Yarn needle

1 – ¾" (2cm) Magnetic snap

Lining: cotton fabric 8½" (21.5cm) wide x 17" (43.25cm) high

Pocket lining: cotton fabric 4" (10cm) wide x 4" (10cm) high

**Finished Measurements**

12" (30.5cm) wide x 8¾" (22.25cm) high

**Finished Measurements Petit Alternate**

8" (20.25cm) wide x 8" (20.25cm) high

**Gauge**

6 cls and 5½ rows = 4" (10cm) in cluster st.

**Substitution Yarn**

6 balls Classic Elite *Bam Boo Print* 77yds (70m) / 50g (100% bamboo)
Colors: 4995 or 4997

## Caribbean Tote Pattern

**Front and Back** (make 2)

Ch 40.

Row 1: Work 1 cl in 4th ch from hook, \* ch 1, skip 1 ch, work 1 cl in next ch, repeat from \* to end. Turn. (19 cls)

Row 2: Ch 3, skip 1st cl, \* work 1 cl in next ch sp, ch 1, skip next cl, repeat from \* ending with 1 cl under 1st ch-3. Turn. (19 cls)

Rows 3–12: Repeat Row 2, 10 times.

Fasten off. Weave in all ends.

### Finishing

With (WS) tog, sew sides and bottoms tog. Sew handles on either side with yarn.

### One-Piece Folded Lining (*see purse lining basics p. 26*)

Measure width and height of finished purse. Cut fabric the actual width + ½" (1.25cm) for seam allowance, and twice the height + 1" (2.5cm) for top seam and fold. If your purse is the same size as given finished measurements, trim should measure:

12" (30.5cm) wide + ½" (1.25cm) = 12½" (31.75cm) wide

[8¾" (22.25cm) high x 2] + 1" (2.5cm) = 18½" (47cm) high

For the pocket, cut fabric 7" (17.75cm) wide x 5¾" (14.5cm) high. For the side and bottom edges, with (WS) facing, fold over ¼" (6mm) and iron. For top edge, with (WS) facing, fold over ¼" (6mm) and iron. Then, fold over ¼" (6mm) and iron again. Hand stitch the top edge with a blind stitch. With the (RS) facing, pin the pocket to the lining. Position the top of the pocket 1" (2.5cm) from the top

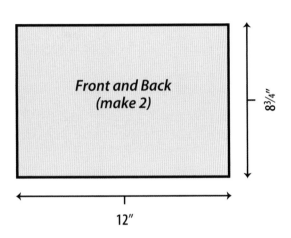

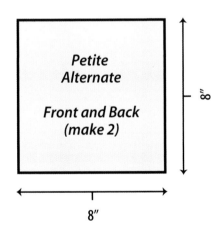

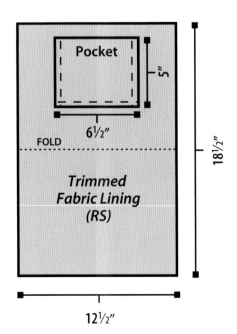

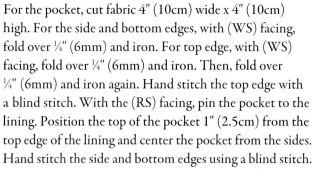

TOP EDGE

**Folded Sewn Lining (WS)**

FOLD

9¼"

12½"

edge of the lining and center the pocket from the sides. Hand stitch the side and bottom edges using a blind stitch.

For the lining, fold in half lengthwise (RS) tog to: 12½" (31.75cm) wide x 9¼" (23.5cm) high. Sew tog along side seams leaving ¼" (6mm) seam allowance. Fold top edge over ½" (1.25cm) on (WS) front and (WS) back and iron. See page 29 for attaching the magnetic snap. Pin the lining to the inside of the bag and hand stitch the top edge using a blind stitch.

## *Caribbean Tote Petit Alternate Pattern*

**Front and Back** (make 2)
Ch 30.

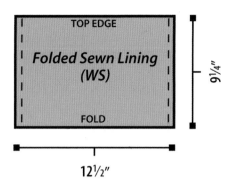

Row 1: Work 1 cl in 4th ch from hook, * ch 1, skip 1 ch, work 1 cl in next ch, repeat from * to end. Turn. (14 cls)

Row 2: Ch 3, skip 1st cl, * work 1 cl in next ch sp, ch 1, skip next cl, repeat from * ending with 1 cl under 1st ch-3. Turn. (14 cls)

Rows 3–12: Repeat Row 2, 10 times.

Fasten off. Weave in all ends.

**Finishing**
With (WS) tog, sew sides and bottoms tog. Sew handles on either side with yarn.

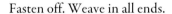

**One-Piece Folded Lining**
*(see purse lining basics p. 26)*
Measure width and height of finished purse. Cut fabric the actual width + ½" (1.25cm) for seam allowance, and twice the height + 1" (2.5cm) for top seam and fold. If your purse is the same size as given finished measurements, trim should measure:

8" (20.25cm) wide + ½" (1.25cm) = 8½" (21.5cm) wide

[8" (20.25cm) high x 2] + 1" (2.5cm) = 17" (43.25cm) high

For the pocket, cut fabric 4" (10cm) wide x 4" (10cm) high. For the side and bottom edges, with (WS) facing, fold over ¼" (6mm) and iron. For top edge, with (WS) facing, fold over ¼" (6mm) and iron. Then, fold over ¼" (6mm) and iron again. Hand stitch the top edge with a blind stitch. With the (RS) facing, pin the pocket to the lining. Position the top of the pocket 1" (2.5cm) from the top edge of the lining and center the pocket from the sides. Hand stitch the side and bottom edges using a blind stitch.

For the lining, fold in half lengthwise (RS) tog to: 8½" (21.5cm) wide x 8½" (21.5cm) high. Sew tog along side seams leaving ¼" (6mm) seam allowance. Fold top edge over ½" (1.25cm) on (WS) front and (WS) back and iron. See page 29 for attaching the magnetic snap. Pin the lining to the inside of the bag and hand stitch the top edge using a blind stitch.

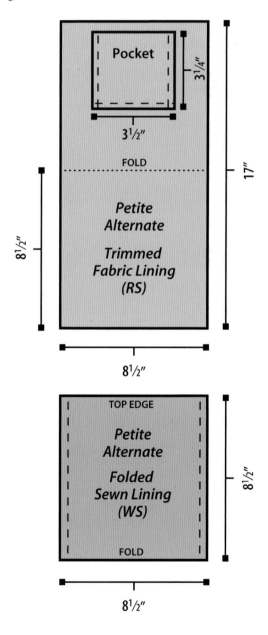

Pocket

3¼"

3½"

FOLD

*Petite Alternate Trimmed Fabric Lining (RS)*

8½"

17"

8½"

TOP EDGE

*Petite Alternate Folded Sewn Lining (WS)*

FOLD

8½"

8½"

# Whimsical Bag

*The unique triangular design of the Whimsical Bag makes crocheting in the round both fun and easy. The lightweight party purse combines supple cotton, which is interwoven with flat ribbon yarn, for that dressed-up look. The weight of the round glass beads creates a natural fold that accentuates the contours of this must-have classic accessory.*

HANDLES  *Crochet*

FABRIC LINING  *Cotton*

EMBELLISH
*Flat Glass Heart Beads*

**Yarns**

A: 2 balls Louisa Harding *Nautical Cotton* 93yds (85m) / 50g (100% mercerized cotton) Color: 03

B: 1 hank Louisa Harding *Sari Ribbon* 66yds (60m) / 50g (90% polyamide, 10% metallic) Color: 07

**Crochet Hook**

US H/8 (5mm) crochet hook, or size needed to obtain gauge.

**Finishing Materials**

55 – Flat glass heart beads

Yarn needle

Sewing needle

Sewing thread

Size B purse insert (Bag-E-Bottom)

Stitch marker

Lining: cotton fabric 10½" (26.75cm) wide x 17" (43.25cm) high

**Finished Measurements**

10" (25cm) wide x 8" (20.25cm) high

**Gauge**

13 sts and 8 rows = approx 4" (10cm) in dc.

**Substitution Yarns**

A: 1 ball Patons *Canadiana* 201yds (184m) / 100g (100% acrylic) Color: 9

B: 1 skein Trendsetter Yarns *Segue Blush* 120yds (110m) / 100g (100% nylon) Color: 300

## *Whimsical Bag Pattern*

**Front or Back**

With A, ch 31.

Rnd 1: Sc in the 2nd ch from hook and in each ch across. (30 sc in this part) Turn chain so the bottom unused lps are at the top. Ch 1. Work 1 sc in each of the unused lps. You are working in rnds. (30 sc in this part: 60 total sc in this rnd.) Join with sl st. PM on the sl st. Move marker up as you complete a rnd. Make sure you do not work a st in sl st at the end of the previous rnd.

Rnd 2: Ch 1, * sc in each of the next 29 sc, 5 sc in last sc. Repeat from *. Join with sl st to 1st sc. (68 sts)

Rnd 3: Ch 1, * sc in each of the next 29 sc, 2 sc in each of the next 5 sc. Repeat from *. Join with sl st to 1st sc. Base of the bag is complete. (78 sts)

Rnd 4: Ch 3, (counts as a dc) dc in each of the next 8 sc, ch 2, skip 2 sc, dc in each of the next 10 sc, ch 2, skip 2 sc, dc in each of the next 24 sc, ch 2, skip 2 sc, dc in each of the next 10 sc, ch 2, skip 2 sc, dc in each of the next 17 sc. Join with sl st to the top ch of 1st ch-3. (70 dc)

Rnds 5–16: Ch 3, dc in each of the next 8 dc, ch 2, skip ch-2 sp, dc in each of the next 10 dc, ch 2, skip ch-2 sp, dc in each of the next 24 dc, ch 2, skip ch-2 sp, dc in each of the next 10 dc, ch 2, skip ch-2 sp, dc in each of the next 17 dc. Join with sl st to the top ch of 1st ch-3. (70 dc)

Fasten off.

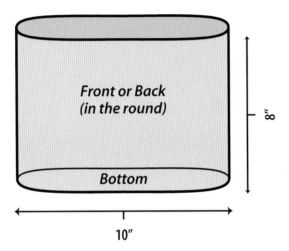

## Edging

With B, join with a sl st to the 1st st of Rnd 16. Work 1 sc in each st around.

## Handle (make 2)

With B, leave a tail long enough to tie a bow and ch 50. Sl st in each ch across. Fasten off, leaving another long tail.

## Finishing

Connect another long length of B to the other end of the handle. Tie handles in a neat bow into ch 2 sps of Rnd 16.

## Weaving Ribbon

Cut four 20" (50.75cm) pieces of ribbon and weave in and out of ch 2 sps. Tie tog on (WS).

## Beading

Sew coordinating beads on Rnd 16. Weave in all ends. Push sides in to create a triangular shape.

## One-Piece Folded Lining (see purse lining basics p. 26)

Measure width and height of finished purse. Cut fabric the actual width + ½" (1.25cm) for the seam allowance, and twice the height + 1" (2.5cm) for the top seam and fold. If your purse is the same size as the given finished measurements, trim should measure:

10" (25cm) wide + ½" (1.25cm) = 10½" (26.75cm) wide

[8" (20.25cm) high x 2] + 1" (2.5cm) = 17" (43.25cm) high

Fold in half lengthwise (RS) tog to: 10½" (26.75cm) wide x 8½" (21.5cm) high. Sew tog along the side seam leaving a ¼" (6mm) seam allowance. Fold top edge over ½" (1.25cm) on (WS) front and (WS) back and iron. Pin the lining to the inside of the bag and hand stitch the top edge using a blind stitch.

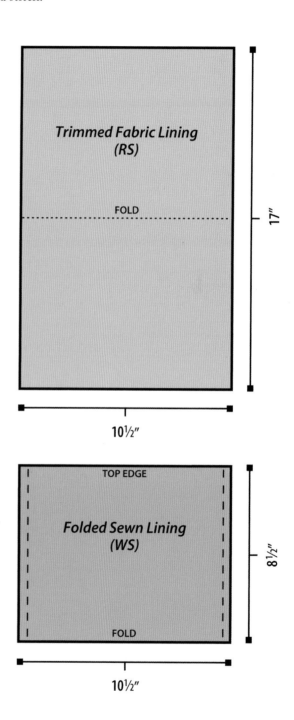

## EASY

# Drawstring Shell Carryall

*The unique drawstring design and the beautiful shell stitch make this bag an extraordinary fashion accessory. The pear-shaped design uses soft cotton and acrylic yarns to create that toss-it-over-the-shoulder design. A sturdy canvas strap and cotton lining complete the all-purpose sling for that casual, laid-back look.*

HANDLES *Canvas Strap*

FABRIC LINING *Cotton*

EMBELLISH *Cord Stop*

**Yarn**

6 balls Plymouth Yarn *Bella Colour* 104yds (95m) / 50g (55% cotton, 45% acrylic)
Color: 16

**Crochet Hook**

US J/10 (6mm) crochet hook, or size needed to obtain gauge.

**Finishing Materials**

1 – 21" (53.25cm) Canvas strap (Dritz)

1 – Cord stop (Dritz)

Yarn needle

Lining: cotton fabric 39" (99cm) wide x 18½" (47cm) high and 12½" (31.75cm) diameter circle

Pocket lining: cotton fabric 6½" (16.5cm) wide x 7¾" (19.75cm) high

**Finished Measurements**

12" (30.5cm) diameter of bottom circle and 18½" (47cm) high

**Gauge**

4 sts and 6 rows = 4" (10cm) in shell stitch pattern.

**Substitution Yarn**

A: 6 balls Gedifra *California Color* 105yds (96m) / 50g (55% cotton, 45% acrylic)
Color: 3177

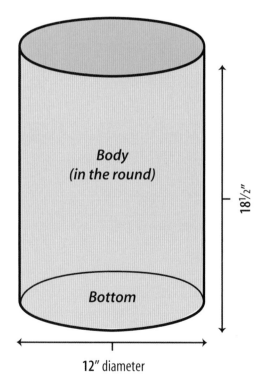

**Body (in the round)**

**Bottom**

18½"

12" diameter

# Drawstring Shell Carryall Pattern

## Bottom

With A, ch 5. Join with sl st in 1st ch to form ring.

Rnd 1: (RS) Ch 3 (does not count as dc here and throughout), 15 dc in center of ring. Join with sl st in top of ch-3. (15 dc) Do not turn.

Rnd 2: Ch 3, 2 dc in each of the next 15 dc. Join with sl st in top of ch-3. (30 dc)

Rnd 3: Ch 3, * 1 dc in 1st dc, 2 dc in next dc, repeat from * around. Join with sl st in top of ch-3. (45 dc)

Rnd 4: Ch 3, * 1 dc in each of the next 2 dc, 2 dc in next dc, repeat from * around. Join with sl st in top of ch-3. (60 dc)

Rnd 5: Ch 3, * 1 dc in each of the next 3 dc, 2 dc in next dc, repeat from * around. Join with sl st in top of ch-3. (75 dc)

Rnd 6: Ch 3, * 1 dc in each of the next 4 dc, 2 dc in next dc, repeat from * around. Join with sl st in top of ch-3. (90 dc)

Rnd 7: Ch 3, * 1 dc in each of the next 5 dc, 2 dc in next dc, repeat from * around. Join with sl st in top of ch-3. (105 dc)

Rnd 8: Ch 3, * 1 dc in each of the next 6 dc, 2 dc in next dc, repeat from * around. Join with sl st in top of ch-3. (120 dc)

## Body

Rnd 9: Ch 1, sc in next dc, * ch 3, 3 dc in same st. Skip 3 sts, 1 sc in next st, repeat from * around for a total of 30 shells. Join with sl st in 1st sc of rnd. (30 shells)

Rnds 10–38: * Ch 1, sc, ch 3, 3 dc in next ch-3 sp, repeat from * around. Join with sl st in 1st sc of rnd. At the end of Rnd 38, fasten off.

## Drawstring

Ch 200. Sl st in each ch to the end. Fasten off. Weave in all ends.

## Finishing

Where the rnds have been joined, sew 1 end of the shoulder strap between Rnds 8 and 9, and the other end between Rnds 34 and 35. Weave drawstring through the shells on Rnd 35, 4 rows from the top. Slide cord stop on drawstring to cinch so that the drawstring ends are opposite from the strap. Weave in all ends.

## Cylinder Lining *(see purse lining basics p. 26)*

Measure the bottom diameter and height of finished purse. For bottom, cut fabric in a circle, the actual diameter of the bottom of the purse + ½" (1.25cm) for seam allowance. For the body height, cut fabric the actual height of the purse x the circumference width + 1" (2.5cm) for side seam allowance. To find the circumference width measure the finished purse around the perimeter.

If your purse is the same size as the given finished measurements, trim should measure:

### Bottom

Bottom circle: 12" (30.5cm) diameter + ½" (1.25cm) = 12½" (31.75cm) diameter

### Body

Body height: 18½" (47cm) high

Body width: 38" (96.5cm) circumference width + 1" (2.5cm) = 39" (99cm) width

For the pocket, cut fabric 6½" (16.5cm) wide x 7¾" (19.75cm) high. For the side and bottom edges, with (WS) facing, fold over ¼" (6mm) and iron. For the top edge, with (WS) facing, fold over ¼" (6mm) and iron. Then, fold over ¼" (6mm) and iron again. Hand stitch the top edge with a blind stitch. With the (RS) facing, pin the pocket to the lining. Position the top of the pocket 2" (5cm) from the top edge of the lining and center the pocket side edges. Hand stitch the side and bottom edges using a blind stitch.

For the body lining, fold in half widthwise (RS) tog to: 19½" (49.5cm) wide x 18½" (47cm) high. Sew 1 side seam tog along side leaving a ¼" (6mm) seam allowance on both sides.

For the bottom circle lining, fold in half and mark the fold with pins. Fold in half in the opposite direction and mark the fold with pins. Repeat for the body. Align the bottom circle

and bottom of body edge tog and pin tog. Sew around seam edge of circle bottom leaving ¼" (6mm) seam allowance.

Fold the top edge over until it fits under the drawstring on (WS) around circumference and iron. Pin the lining to the inside of the bag under the drawstring and hand stitch the top edge using a blind stitch.

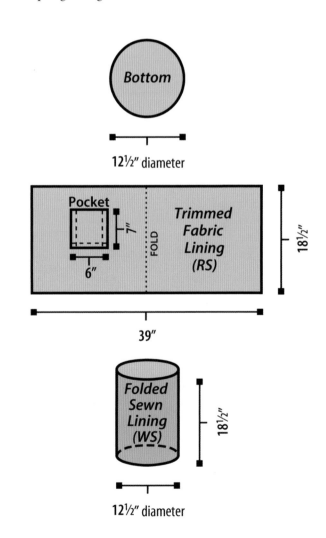

# Ice Princess Purse

*You'll feel royal sporting this vinyl Ice Princess Purse while showing off the glossy texture of super-cool Ice Jelly Yarn. This quick-to-crochet, hip evening bag features an adorable ruffle with multiple rows of blue beads. The clear U-shaped handles are the perfect match. You'll look hot, yet be cool with this classic look-at-me accessory.*

HANDLES *Clear U-shaped*

FABRIC LINING *Vinyl*

EMBELLISH *Blue E Beads*

### Yarn

2 balls Jelly Yarn® *Ice Fine* 85yds (78m) / 200g (100% vinyl) Color: Ice

### Crochet Hook

US I /9 (5.5mm) crochet hook, or size needed to obtain gauge.

### Finishing Materials

900 – Blue E beads

2 – Clear U-shaped handles

¼ yd (.25m) Vinyl

Yarn needle

Lining: vinyl material 7" (17.75cm) wide x 13" (33cm) high

Pocket lining: vinyl material 3½" (9cm) wide x 3½" (9cm) high

### Finished Measurements

6½" (16.5cm) wide x 6½" (16.5cm) high

### Gauge

16 sts and 12 rows = 4" (10cm) in 1 row sc, 1 row dc.

### Substitution Yarn

2 balls Jelly Yarn® *Honey Gold Fine* 85yds (78m) / 200g (100% vinyl) Color: Honey Gold

*Single Crochet (sc)*

*Double Crochet (dc)*

SPECIAL STITCH

*Beaded Single Crochet (bsc)*

Slip the bead close to the hook, insert the hook into the st indicated, yo, pull through the st. Yo and pull through 2 lps. Push the beads through to the (RS).

## Ice Princess Purse Pattern

**Front and Back** (make 2)

String all beads before beginning.

With Ice, ch 26.

Row 1: (RS) Slip a bead close to hook. Work 1 sc in 2nd ch from hook, making sure you push the bead to the front each time, * slip bead, work 1 sc in next st *. Repeat from * to end. Turn. (25 beaded sc)

Row 2: (WS) Ch 1, work beaded sc in 1st beaded sc of previous row and each st across. All beads should be on (RS). Turn. (25 beaded sc)

Row 3: Ch 1, * slip bead, sc in 1st beaded sc, slip bead, sc in next beaded sc *. Repeat from * across. All beads should be on (RS). Turn.

Row 4: Repeat Row 2.

Row 5: Ch 3 (counts as 1st dc here and throughout). Skip 1st beaded sc, dc in next beaded sc and in each st across. Turn. (25 dc)

Rows 6–15: Repeat Rows 4 and 5, 5 more times.

Row 16: Repeat Row 4, 1 more time.

Row 17: Ch 3. 3 dc in 1st beaded sc, * 4 dc in next beaded sc. Repeat from * across. (100 dc, counting the 1st ch-3)

Row 18: Ch 1, work 1 beaded sc with 2 beads in 1st dc and each dc across. Fasten off.

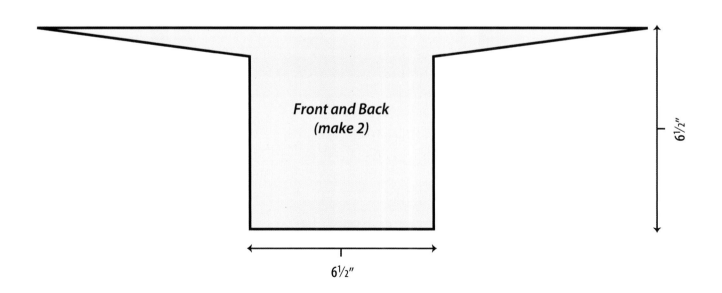

**Front and Back**
**(make 2)**

6½"

6½"

For the lining, fold in half lengthwise (RS) tog to: 7" (17.75cm) wide x 6½" (16.5cm) high.

Sew tog along the side seams leaving a ¼" (6mm) seam allowance. Pin the lining to the inside of the bag and hand stitch the top edge using monofilament thread.

## Finishing

Using Ice, sew 2 pieces with (WS) tog. Leave top open. With Ice, sew U-shaped handles to last dc row on the inside of bag. Weave in all ends.

**One-Piece Folded Lining** *(see purse lining basics p. 26)*
Measure the width and the height of the finished purse. Cut fabric the actual width + ½" (1.25cm) for the seam allowance, and twice the height. If your purse is the same size as the given finished measurements, trim should measure:

6½" (16.5cm) wide + ½" (1.25cm) = 7" (17.75cm) wide

6½" (16.5cm) high x 2 = 13" (33cm) high

For the pocket, cut vinyl 3½" (9cm) wide x 3½" (9cm) high. Position 1" (2.5cm) from top and center on (RS) facing of lining and sew zigzag st for the side and bottom edges.

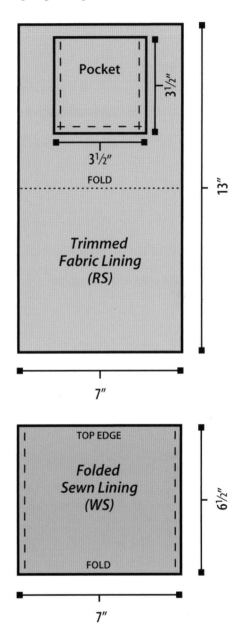

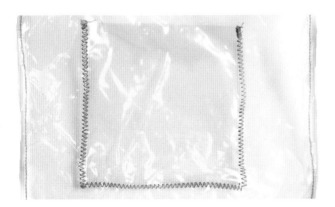

# Petals Purse

*Small in size, yet large in appeal, this casual purse features a uniquely designed petal stitch pattern. Cotton and acrylic fibers surround the bag with a harmony of colorful, soft petals. Funky swirl handles and a vertical striped lining make the Petals Purse a one-of-a-kind design. You'll enjoy carrying this fun bag around all year.*

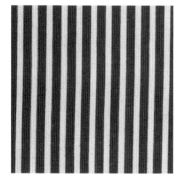

HANDLES *Swirl*

## Yarn

4 balls GGH *Illusion* 65yds (59m) / 50g (34% cotton, 33% acetate, 33% acrylic)
Color: 006

## Crochet Hooks

US G/6 (4mm) and US I/9 (5.5mm) crochet hooks, or size needed to obtain gauge.

## Finishing Materials

2 – Swirl handles

Stitch markers

Yarn needle

Lining: cotton fabric – 2 Bottom ovals 10" (25cm) long diameter x 4½" (11cm) short diameter

Lining: cotton fabric – 2 Sides/Body 23½" (59.75cm) wide x 6" (15cm) high

## Finished Measurements

9½" (24cm) wide x 5" (12.75cm) high

## Gauge

16 sts and 6 rows = 4" (10cm) in dc.

## Substitution Yarn

3 balls Needful Yarns *Korallo* 90yds (82m) / 50g (45% cotton, 43% acrylic, 12% nylon) Color: 201

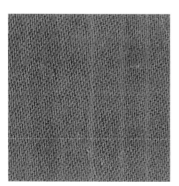

FABRIC LINING   *Cotton (Inner)*

FABRIC LINING   *Cotton (Outer)*

## Petals Purse Pattern

### STITCHES USED

*Slip Stitch (sl st)*

*Single Crochet (sc)*

*Double Crochet (dc)*

*Treble Crochet (tr)*

*Double Treble Crochet (dtr)*

### SPECIAL STITCH

*Petal Stitch*

(1 sc, 1 dc, 1 tr, 1 dtr, 1 tr, 1 dc, 1 sc) in ch-2 sp.

*Note: Move markers with each rnd.*

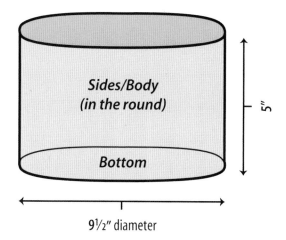

Sides/Body (in the round)

Bottom

5"

9½" diameter

### Bottom

With I/9 (5.5mm) hook, ch 23.

Rnd 1: 5 dc in 4th ch from hook (PM in last dc of this group), dc in each of next 18 chs, 6 dc in last ch (PM in 1st and last dc of this group). Working along the bottom side of the ch, in the unused lps, dc in each of next 18 chs. Join with a sl st to top ch of 1st ch-3. DO NOT TURN. (48 dc, including 1st ch-3)

Rnd 2: Ch 3, dc in same st as joining, 2 dc in each of next 5 dc until marker, dc in each of next 18 dc until next marker, 2 dc in each of next 6 dc until marker, dc in each of next 18 dc until end of rnd. Join with sl st to top ch of 1st ch-3. DO NOT TURN. (60 dc, including 1st ch-3)

Rnd 3: Ch 3, dc in same st as joining. Dc in next dc, * 2 dc in next dc, dc in next dc. Repeat from * 4 more times, until marker. Dc in each of next 18 dc until next marker, ** 2 dc in next dc, dc in next dc. Repeat from ** 5 more times, until next marker. Dc in each of next 18 dc until end of rnd. Join with sl st in top ch of 1st ch-3. DO NOT FASTEN OFF. (72 dc, including 1st ch-3)

### Sides / Body

Change to G/6 (4mm) hook.

Rnd 1: Ch 5 (counts as dc, ch 2 here and throughout), skip 3 dc, dc in next dc. * Ch 2, skip 2 dc, dc in next dc. Repeat from * around, ending with ch 2, join with sl st in 3rd ch of 1st ch-5. (24 dc, inc 1st ch-3)

Rnds 2–10: Ch 5, * dc in next dc, ch 2. Repeat from * around, ending with ch 2, join with sl st in 3rd ch of 1st ch-5.

Fasten off after Rnd 10.

### Petals

Begin where the bottom meets the side.

Rnd 1: Attach yarn with a sc to any ch-2 on Rnd 1 of side. Work petal st in each ch-2 sp around. Join with sl st in 1 sc of 1st petal. Fasten off.

Repeat this rnd for all odd numbered rnds of side. Fasten off after every rnd.

## Finishing

Fold purse flat. Slip handles under the top row of ch-2 sps between 2 dc and adjust the spacing so that the purse hangs evenly from the handles. Using yarn and a yarn needle, secure the handles by sewing tog the 2 adjacent dc. Weave in all ends.

### Cylinder Lining *(see purse lining basics p. 26)*

Because the purse is created in an openwork crochet pattern, this purse has a double lining of fabric (WS) to (WS). Pin 2 pieces of 6" (15.25cm) wide x 11" (28cm) long fabric with (WS) tog. Center the purse bottom on the (RS) of the fabric and trace around the oval. Circumference of the bottom oval should be 23" (58.5cm) For the bottom, cut a fabric oval and add ½" (1.25cm). This means ¼" (6mm) will be around the circumference for the seam allowance. If your purse is the same size as the given finished measurements, trim should measure:

*Bottom Oval* (make 2)

9½" (24cm) long diameter + ½" (1.25cm) = 10" (25cm) wide

4" (10cm) short diameter + ½" (1.25cm) = 4½" (11cm) high

For the sides/body, cut fabric the actual height of the purse plus 1" (2.5cm) for the top seam and fold x the width, the circumference of the oval bottom + ½" (1.25cm) for the bottom seam allowance. If your purse is the same size as the given finished measurements, trim should measure:

*Sides/Body* (make 2)

5" (12.75cm) high + 1" (2.5cm) = 6" (15cm) high

23" (58.5cm) wide + ½" (1.25cm) = 23½" (59.75cm) wide

For the sides/body, fold in half widthwise, (RS) tog 6" (15cm) high x 11¾" (30cm) wide and sew ¼" (6mm) seam allowance. Repeat for 2nd side lining. You now have 2 tube linings.

For the bottom oval linings, fold in half and mark the fold with pins. Fold in half in the opposite direction and mark the fold with pins. Repeat for the sides/body. Align the bottom oval and bottom of side edge tog and pin tog. Sew around seam edge of oval bottom leaving ¼" (6mm) seam allowance. Repeat for 2nd side lining. You now have 2 purse linings.

Place one lining inside the other with (RS) tog. Sew ¼" (6mm) around top edge leaving a 3" (7.5cm) opening so you can turn it inside out. Turn the linings inside out and sew opening closed by hand. Place inside crochet bag and sew top edge all around circumference of bag using a blind stitch.

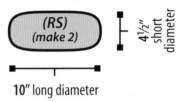

**Trimmed Fabric Lining  Bottom Oval**

(RS)
(make 2)

4½" short diameter

10" long diameter

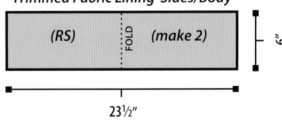

**Trimmed Fabric Lining  Sides/Body**

(RS) FOLD (make 2)

6"

23½"

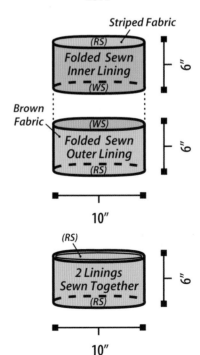

Striped Fabric

(RS)
**Folded Sewn Inner Lining**
(WS)

6"

Brown Fabric

(WS)
**Folded Sewn Outer Lining**
(RS)

6"

10"

(RS)
**2 Linings Sewn Together**
(RS)

6"

10"

# 3
# Fall and Winter Handbags

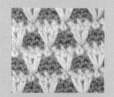

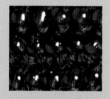

Cool weather handbags feature deep rich colors and crocheted textures with plush seasonal fibers. Cotton, soft alpaca, silk, suede, mohair, and wool yarns are perfect compliments for fall and winter styles. This collection of handbags reflects the deep colors and rich textures suitable for any fashion setting. There are designs to fit any lifestyle or occasion; working, shopping, travel, or evening wear.

Begin with an embellished overlay stitch featured in the small Striped Demi Bag. The Nautical Shoulder Bag and Grace Purse are simple box constructions using special decorative stitches. The Shell Sack is worked in two colors and has a tri-color alternate version. If you prefer a larger bag, carry all your essentials in the Harlequin Barrel Bag. The Beaded Evening Purse is a chic feminine design, ideal for that special occasion. For a unique textural fabric, the Satchel utilizes two merino wool yarn colors. The Tunisian knit stitch is a perfect texture for the nifty Messenger Bag. Enjoy the diversity of styles that these handbags offer for any occasion.

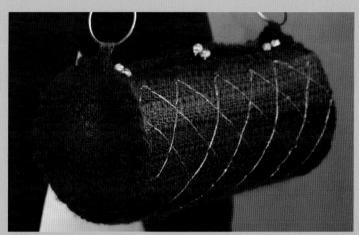

**BEGINNER**

# Striped Demi Bag

*The mini tri-color striped bag, an easy first purse to crochet, is created from two identical pieces. Three cotton yarn colors create this color-coordinated bag, featuring a simple overlay stitch technique. Sew seams and add wood purse handles to complete this quick-to-finish bag. It's small in size yet big enough for all the essentials.*

HANDLES *Wood with Rings*

FABRIC LINING *Cotton*

### Yarns

A: 2 balls Louisa Harding *Nautical Cotton* 93yds (85m) / 50g (100% mercerized cotton) Color: 2

B: 1 ball Louisa Harding *Nautical Cotton* 93yds (85m) / 50g (100% mercerized cotton) Color: 13

C: 1 ball Louisa Harding *Nautical Cotton* 93yds (85m) / 50g (100% mercerized cotton) Color: 14

### Crochet Hook

US H/8 (5mm) crochet hook, or size needed to obtain gauge.

### Finishing Materials

2 – Wood purse handles with rings (Bag Boutique™)

Yarn needle

Lining: cotton fabric 6½" (16.5cm) wide x 14½" (36.75cm) high

### Finished Measurements (without handles)

6" (15.25cm) wide x 6¾" (17cm) high

### Gauge

16 sts and 19 rows = 4" (10cm) in sc.

### Substitution Yarns

A: 1 ball Patons *Canadiana* 201yds (184m) / 100g (100% acrylic) Color: 31

B: 1 ball Patons *Canadiana* 201yds (184m) / 100g (100% acrylic) Color: 01

C: 1 ball Patons *Canadiana* 201yds (184m) / 100g (100% acrylic) Color: 81

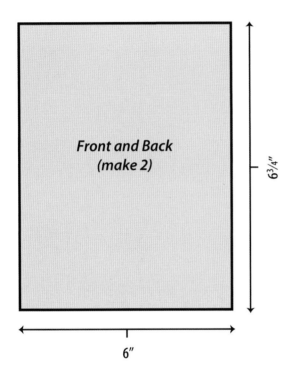

Front and Back
(make 2)

6¾"

6"

 *Striped Demi Bag Pattern*

**Front and Back** (make 2)
With B, ch 31.

Row 1: (RS) Sc in 2nd ch from hook and in each ch across. Change to C. Turn.

Row 2: (WS) Ch 1, sc in each st to end. Change to A. Turn.

Rows 3–4: Ch 1, sc in each st to end. Turn.

Row 5: Ch 1, sc in each st to end. Change to B. Turn.

Row 6: Ch 1, sc in each st to end. Change to C. Turn.

Rows 7–26: Repeat Rows 2–6, 4 more times. At the end of Row 26, Change to C. Turn.

Row 27: Ch 1 sc in each st to end. Fasten off.

Row 28: Join B with sl st to beg of Row 27. Ch 1, sc in each st across to end. Fasten off.

**Overlay Chain Stitch**
With B, working on (RS) of front, insert hook 4 sts in from bottom end. Work overlay st across bottom of purse to end Fasten off.

With C, insert hook 5 sts in from same end. Work overlay st across bottom of purse, 1 stitch above B, to the end. Fasten off.

With A, insert hook 6 sts in from same end. Work overlay st across bottom of purse, 1 st above C, to the end. Fasten off.

Repeat for back.

## Finishing

Slide crocheted fabric into handle slit. Fold over wood on (WS) of fabric. With A, sew flap to (WS). Repeat for the 2nd handle. With (WS) tog, sew edges all around. For easier opening, begin sewing 1" (2.5cm) below handles. Weave in all ends.

**One-Piece Folded Lining** *(see purse lining basics p. 26)*
Measure width and height of finished purse. Cut fabric the actual width + ½" (1.25cm) for the seam allowance and twice the height plus 1" (2.5cm) for the top seam and fold. If your purse is the same size as the given finished measurements, trim should measure:

6" (15.25cm) wide + ½" (1.25cm) = 6½" (16.5cm) wide

[6¾" (17cm) high x 2] + 1" (2.5cm) = 14½" (36.75cm) high

Fold in half lengthwise (RS) tog to: 6½" (16.5cm) wide x 7¼" (18.5cm) high. Sew tog along the side seams leaving a ¼" (6mm) seam allowance. Fold top edge over ½" (1.25cm) on (WS) front and (WS) back and iron. Pin the lining to the inside of the bag and hand stitch the top edge using a blind stitch.

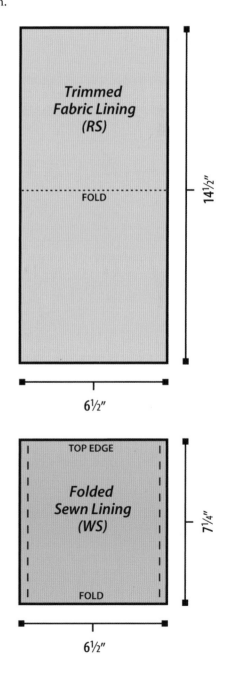

Trimmed Fabric Lining (RS)

FOLD

14½"

6½"

TOP EDGE

Folded Sewn Lining (WS)

7¼"

FOLD

6½"

# Nautical Shoulder Bag

*The patriotic red, white, and blue nautical bag features front post double crochet stitches to create an elevated, ribbed look. Colorful suede and silk yarns make this casual companion easy to crochet and fun to carry. Silver buttons and a sturdy canvas lining accentuate the appeal of this sporty-looking purse.*

HANDLES *Vinyl Strap*

FABRIC LINING *Poplin*

EMBELLISH *Silver Star Buttons*

## Yarns

A: 4 balls Berroco *Suede* 120yds (110m) / 50g (100% nylon) Color: 3704 Wrangler

B: 1 ball Berroco *Ultra Silk* 98yds (90m) / 50g (40% rayon, 40% nylon, 20% silk) Color: 6101 Ivory

C: 1 ball Berroco *Ultra Silk* 98yds (90m) / 50g (40% rayon, 40% nylon, 20% silk) Color: 6115 Cinnabar

## Crochet Hook

US H/8 (5mm) crochet hook, or size needed to obtain gauge.

## Finishing Materials

2 – 9" (22.75cm) x 10" (25cm) Plastic needlepoint canvas

3 – 2½" (6.25cm) x 10" (25cm) Plastic needlepoint canvas

1 – 22½" (57.25cm) white vinyl strap

3 – Velcro® tabs

5 – Silver star buttons

Yarn needle

Sewing needle and thread

Lining: poplin fabric – 2 Front and Sides 14" (35.5cm) wide x 14¾" (37.5cm) high

Lining: poplin fabric – 2 Back and Sides 14" (35.5cm) wide x 14¾" (37.5cm) high

## Finished Measurements

10½" (26.75cm) wide x 10½" (26.75cm) high x 3" (7.5cm) deep

## Gauge

16 sts and 20 rows = 4" (10cm) in dc.

## Substitution Yarns

A: 6 balls Louisa Harding *Fauve* 87yds (80m) / 50g (100% nylon) Color: 14

B: 1 ball Gedifra *Colorito* 103yds (94m) / 50g (52% nylon, 25% rayon, 23% cotton) Color: 6944

C: 1 ball Gedifra *Colorito* 103yds (94m) / 50g (52% nylon, 25% rayon, 23% cotton) Color: 6925

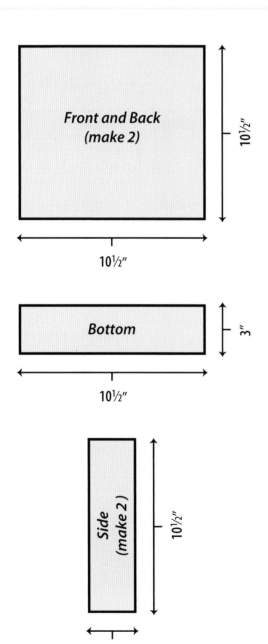

 *Nautical Shoulder Bag Pattern*

**Front and Back** (make 2)

With A, ch 43.

Row 1: Dc in 4th ch from hook and in each ch across. Turn. (41 dc, including 1st ch-3)

Row 2 (RS): Ch 1. Sc in 1st dc, FPdc around each of next 3 dc, * sc in each of next 3 dc, FPdc around each of next 3 dc. Repeat from * across, ending sc in top ch of 1st ch-3. Turn. (21 FPdc, 20 sc)

Row 3: Ch 1. Sc in each st across. (41 sc) Turn.

Row 4: Ch 1. Sc in 1st sc, FPdc around each of next 3 FPdc in Row 2, * sc in each of next 3 sc, FPdc around each of next 3 FPdc in Row 2. Repeat from * across, ending sc in last sc. Turn.

Rows 5–46: Repeat Rows 3 and 4, working the FPdc in each (RS) row around the FPdc in the previous (RS) row.

Fasten off after Row 46. Weave in all ends.

**Side** (make 2)

With A, ch 13.

Row 1: Dc in 4th ch from hook and in each ch across. Turn. (11 dc, including 1st ch-3)

Row 2: Repeat Row 2 of front and back. Turn. (6 FPdc, 5 sc)

Row 3: Repeat Row 3 of front and back. Turn. (11 sc)

Row 4: Repeat Row 4 of front and back. Turn.

Rows 5–46: Repeat Rows 3 and 4, working the FPdc in each (RS) row around the FPdc in the previous (RS) row.

Fasten off after Row 46. Weave in all ends.

**Bottom**

With A, ch 13.

Rows 1–46: Repeat directions for Rows 1–46 of Side. Fasten off. Weave in all ends.

**Finishing**

With A, and (WS) tog, whipstitch, through the inner lps, the front, back, sides, and bottom tog to form a rectangular box.

**Edging**

Row 1: Attach B with a sl st to a corner of the bag. Sc in each st around the top of bag. Join with sl st to 1st sc. DO NOT TURN.

Row 2: Ch 1, sc in each st around. Join with sl st to 1st sc. DO NOT TURN.

Rows 3–5: Repeat Row 2. Change to C.

Row 6: Ch 1, * sc in 1st sc, ch 3, skip 1 sc, 3 dc in next sc. Repeat from * around. Join with sl st to 1st sc. Fasten off.

### Inside Flap

With (WS) tog, mark center 31 sts along Row 46 (last Row using Yarn A) of back of bag. Join A at 1st marker.

Row 1: Sc in each st to next marker. Turn.

Row 2: Ch 3, skip 1st sc, dc in each st across. Turn.

Rows 3–6: Repeat row 2.

Row 7: Ch 1, sc in each st across. Fasten off.

### Box / Gusset Lining

*(see purse lining basics p. 27)*
For the lining, the plastic needlepoint canvas acts as a support for the purse. You will be assembling the plastic canvas pieces to form a support box, then make the fabric lining to fit inside the box. Use the finished crocheted purse as a visual guide when making the support box.

Use the five plastic canvas pieces tog to form a box. Tape the pieces tog to form a support box with an open end. Position this in your finished purse and check the fit. If the support box is too large, trim pieces to fit. Whipstitch adjoining edges tog with yarn.

Cut fabric for the front, back, and sides the actual width + ½" (1.25cm) for the side seam allowance. For the height, use the actual height plus 1" (2.5cm) for the bottom, ¼" (6mm) for bottom seam allowance and 3" (7.5cm) for the top fold.

If your purse is the same size as the given finished measurements, trim should measure:

*Front and Side*

10½" (26.75cm) + 3" (7.5cm) wide + ½" (1.25cm) = 14" (35.5cm) wide

10½" (26.75cm) high + 3" (7.5cm) + ¼" (6mm) + 1" (2.5cm) = 14¾" (37.5cm) high

*Back and Side*

10½" (26.75cm) + 3" (7.5cm) wide + ½" (1.25cm) = 14" (35.5cm) wide

10½" (26.75cm) high + 3" (7.5cm)+ ¼" (6mm) + 1" (2.5cm) = 14¾" (37.5cm) high

To make both sides of the box, with (RS) facing, fold a 3" (7.5cm) flap from the left edge. Front and back should measure 11" (28cm) wide x 14¾" (37.5cm) high. Sew

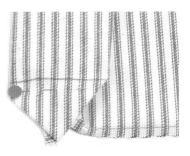

down side seams to form a box. Then, sew across bottom leaving ¼" (6mm) allowance. To create flat bottom, open edges of side seam and iron. The fabric comes to a point in the corner. Sew a seam 1½" (3.75cm) from point. Repeat for other side. Turn (WS) out. Place the lining inside the plastic support box. Fold top edge of fabric over top edge of plastic and sew in place. Insert the lined plastic box in the finished crochet purse and hand sew the top edges of lining to bag with a needle and thread using a blind stitch.

### Extra Finishing Materials

Sew handles to either side of the bag just below the 1st rnd of the edging. Attach 5 star buttons vertically down the center FPdc on the front of the bag. Align Velcro® tabs, evenly spaced, to the flap and inside of the bag, and sew in place.

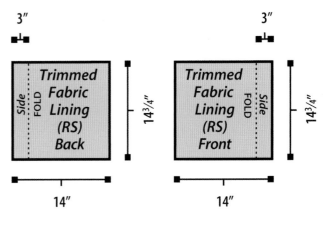

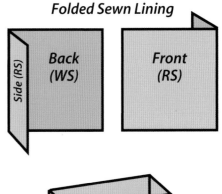

**EASY**

# Grace Purse

*Create this sassy bag with a popular arch lace stitch. Crocheted with soft nylon yarns, this must-have fashion accessory ties on both sides and features large, twisted amber handles. Four crocheted roses, placed at the base of the handles, embellish this adorable purse. It's ideal for a day of shopping or a night on the town.*

HANDLES *Plastic Twist*

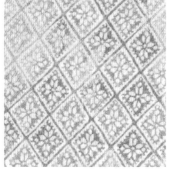

FABRIC LINING *Cotton*

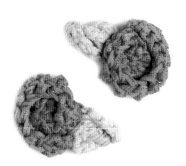

EMBELLISH *Crochet Roses and Leaves*

## Yarns

A: 5 balls Louisa Harding *Fauve* 87yds (80m) / 50g (100% nylon) Color: 8

B: 1 ball Louisa Harding *Fauve* 87yds (80m) / 50g (100% nylon) Color: 18

## Crochet Hook

US G/6 (4mm) crochet hook, or size needed to obtain gauge.

## Finishing Materials

2 – Amber plastic twist handles (Dritz)

Size B purse insert (Bag-E-Bottom)

Yarn needle

1 – ¾" (2cm) Magnetic snap

Stitch marker

Lining: cotton fabric Front and Back 9½" (24cm) wide x 9¼" (23.5cm) high

Lining: cotton fabric – 2 Sides 3⅞" (10cm) wide x 9¼" (23.5cm) high

Lining: cotton fabric Bottom 9½" (24cm) wide x 3⅞" (10cm) high

## Finished Measurements

9" (22.75cm) wide x 8" (20.25cm) high

## Gauge

4 Arch Lace patt st repeats = 4½" (11.5cm) and 11 rows or 5½" patt row repeats = 4" (10cm).

## Substitution Yarns

A: 4 balls Berroco *Suede* 120yds (110m) / 50g (100% nylon) Color: 3757 Clementine

B: 1 ball Berroco *Suede* 120yds (110m) / 50g (100% nylon) Color: 3715 Tonto

Arch Lace Pattern (worked on a multiple of 6 sts)

Row 1: Ch 1, sc in 2nd st, * ch 3, skip 3 sts, sc in each of the next 3 sts. Repeat from * across, ending with sc in each of the next 2 sts. Turn.

Row 2: Ch 1, skip 1st sc, * skip next sc, 5 tr in ch-3 sp, skip sc, sc in next sc. Repeat from * across, ending with sc in ch-1. Turn.

Row 3: Ch 3, skip 1st sc and tr, * sc in each of the next 3 tr, ch 3, skip [tr, sc, tr] repeat from * across, ending with sc in each of the next 3 tr, ch 2, skip tr, sc in ch-1. Turn.

Row 4: Ch 3, (counts as 1st tr), skip 1st sc, 2 tr in ch-2 sp, * skip sc, sc in next sc, skip sc, 5 tr in ch-3 sp. Repeat from * across, ending with 3 tr in ch-3 sp. Turn.

Row 5: Ch 1, skip 1st tr, sc in next tr, * ch 3, skip [tr, sc, tr], sc in each of the next 3 tr, repeat from * across, ending with sc in last tr, sc in top of ch-3. Turn.

Repeat Rows 2–5 for patt.

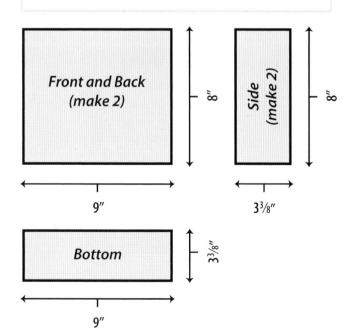

## Grace Purse Pattern

**Roses** (make 4)

You are working in a spiral. Do not turn at end of rnds.

With A, ch 3, sl st in 1st ch to form a ring.

Rnd 1: Ch 2 (does not count as a st), 8 hdc in ring. PM in last hdc.

Rnd 2: In front lp only, dc in each of the next 8 sts. Move marker to last st.

Rnd 3: * Tr in next st, 2 tr in next st, repeat from * to marker. Join with a sl st to 1st tr of rnd. Fasten off.

**Leaf** (make 4)

Join B in any back lp of first 8 hdc from Rnd 1 of rose. Working in the back lp only (DO NOT CH 4), 2 tr in each of the next 2 sts. Fasten off.

**Front and Back** (make 2)

With A, ch 48.

Row 1: Ch 1, sc in 2nd ch from hook, * ch 3, skip 3 chs, sc in each of the next 3 chs. Repeat from * across, ending with sc in each of the next 2 chs. Turn. (24 sc)

Row 2: Ch 1, skip 1st sc, * skip next sc, 5 tr in ch-3 sp, skip sc, sc in next sc. Repeat from * across, ending with sc in ch-1. Turn. (8 tr, 8 sc)

Row 3: Ch 3, skip 1st sc and tr, * sc in each of the next 3 tr, ch 3, skip [tr, sc, tr], repeat from * across, ending with sc in each of the next 3 tr, ch 2, skip tr, sc in ch-1. Turn. (25 sc)

Row 4: Ch 3, (counts as 1st tr), skip 1st sc, 2 tr in ch-2 sp, * skip sc, sc in next sc, skip sc, 5 tr in ch-3 sp. Repeat from * across, ending with 3 tr in ch-3 sp. Turn. (41 tr, 8 sc)

Row 5: Ch 1, skip 1st tr, sc in next tr, * ch 3, skip [tr, sc, tr], sc in each of the next 3 tr, repeat from * across, ending with sc in last tr, sc in top of ch-3. Turn. (24 sc)

Rows 6–21: Repeat Rows 2–5, 4 more times.

**Front and Back (make 2)**

8″

9″

**Side (make 2)**

8″

3⅜″

**Bottom**

3⅜″

9″

## Bottom

With A, ch 18.

Row 1: Ch 1, sc in 2nd ch from hook, * ch 3, skip 3 chs, sc in each of the next 3 chs. Repeat from * ending with sc in each of the next 2 chs. Turn. (9 sc)

Row 2: Ch 1, skip 1st sc, * skip next sc, 5 tr in ch-3 sp, skip sc, sc in next sc. Repeat from *, ending with sc in ch-1. Turn. (3 sc, 15 tr)

Row 3: Ch 3, skip 1st sc and tr, * sc in each of the next 3 tr, ch 3, skip [tr, sc, tr], repeat from *, ending with sc in each of the next 3 tr, ch 2, skip tr, sc in ch-1. Turn. (10 sc)

Row 4: Ch 3, (counts as 1st tr), skip 1st sc, 2 tr in ch-2 sp, * skip sc, sc in next sc, skip sc, 5 tr in ch-3 sp. Repeat from * across, ending with 3 tr in ch-3 sp. Turn. (16 tr, 3 sc)

Row 5: Ch 1, skip 1st tr, sc in next tr, * ch 3, skip [tr, sc, tr], sc in each of the next 3 tr, repeat from *, ending with sc in last tr, sc in top of ch-3. Turn. (9 sc)

Rows 6–21: Repeat Rows 2–5, 4 more times.

Rows 22–23: Repeat Rows 2–3, 1 more time.

## Sides (make 2)

Repeat directions for Bottom for 21 rows.

## Ties for Sides (make 2)

With A and B held tog, ch 100. End off.

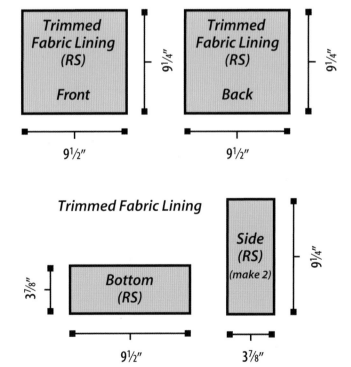

Trimmed Fabric Lining (RS) — Front — 9¼" — 9½"

Trimmed Fabric Lining (RS) — Back — 9¼" — 9½"

**Trimmed Fabric Lining**

Bottom (RS) — 3⅞" — 9½"

Side (RS) (make 2) — 9¼" — 3⅞"

## Finishing

Sew the front, back, sides, and bottom tog with yarn. Sew handles onto the top center edge of the bag. Sew 1 rose at each handle bottom with yarn. Weave ties 2 rows down from the top of the front and back, and tie in place. Place purse insert inside bag and sew to lining bottom. Weave in all ends.

**Box / Gusset Lining** (see purse lining basics p. 27)

Measure width, height, and depth of finished purse. Cut fabric for the front, back, and sides the actual width + ½" (1.25cm) for the side seam allowance, and the actual height plus ¼" (6mm) for the bottom seam and 1" (2.5cm) for the top fold. Cut a piece of fabric for the bottom the actual width and height + ½" (1.25cm) for the side seam allowance. If your purse is the same size as the given finished measurements, trim should measure:

**Front and Back** (make 2)

9" (22.75cm) wide + ½" (1.25cm) = 9½" (24cm) wide

8" (20.25cm) high + 1¼" (3.25cm) = 9¼" (23.5cm) high

**Sides** (make 2)

3⅜" (8.5cm) wide + ½" (1.25cm) = 3⅞" (10cm) wide

8" (20.25cm) high + 1¼" (3.25cm) = 9¼" (23.5cm) high

**Bottom**

9" (22.75cm) wide + ½" (1.25cm) = 9½" (24cm) wide

3⅜" (8.5cm) high + ½" (1.25cm) = 3⅞" (10cm) high

With (RS) tog sew ¼" (6mm) seam for the front and left seam of the side tog. With (RS) tog, sew ¼" (6mm) seam for the back and right seam of the side tog. Sew these 2 units tog with ¼" (6mm) seam to form a fabric tube. With (RS) tog, pin bottom in place and sew to the base of the tube with ¼" (6mm) seam all around. Backstitch to lock in corners.

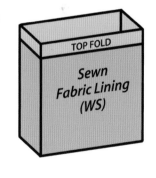

TOP FOLD

Sewn Fabric Lining (WS)

Fold the top edge over ½" (1.25cm) on (WS) front and (WS) back and iron. Fold over ¼" (6mm) again and iron. See page 29 for attaching the magnetic snap. Pin the lining to the inside of the bag and hand stitch the top edge using a blind stitch.

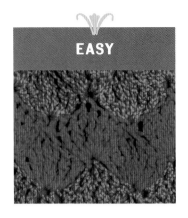

# Shell Sack

*This versatile shoulder sack bag uses a simple shell stitch technique that's fun and easy to make. Two cotton yarns are combined to fashion an attractive carryall that holds everything, yet weighs nothing. Add a red lining and roomy circular handles for that unique, kicked-back casual look. The longer, tri-color alternate version utilizes a medley of three yarn colors. So cool!*

HANDLES *Wooden Circular*

FABRIC LINING *Cotton*

**Yarns**

A: 2 balls Knit One, Crochet Too *Cottonade* 83yds (76m) / 50g (100% cotton) Color: 255 Lipstick

B: 2 balls Knit One, Crochet Too *Cottonade* 83yds (76m) / 50g (100% cotton) Color: 862 Nutmeg

**Yarns Tri-color Alternate**

A: 2 balls Knit One, Crochet Too *Cottonade* 83yds (76m) / 50g (100% cotton) Color: 531 Kiwi

B: 2 balls Knit One, Crochet Too *Cottonade* 83yds (76m) / 50g (100% cotton) Color: 372 Melon

C: 2 balls Knit One, Crochet Too *Cottonade* 83yds (76m) / 50g (100% cotton) Color: 891 Chocolate

**Crochet Hook**

US K/10½ (6.5mm) crochet hook, or size needed to obtain gauge.

**Finishing Materials**

2 – 9" (22.75cm) Wooden circular handles

Yarn needle

Lining: cotton fabric 12½" (31.75cm) wide x 27" (68.5cm) high

**Finishing Materials Tri-color Alternate**

2 – 9" (23cm) Wooden circular handles

Yarn needle

Lining: cotton fabric 12½" (31.75cm) wide x 32" (81.25cm) high

**Finished Measurements**

12" (30.5cm) wide x 12" (30.5cm) high

**Finished Measurements Tri-color Shell Sack**

12" (30.5cm) wide x 14½" (36.75cm) high

**Gauge**

1½" shell sts and 4 rows = 4" (10cm) in shell stitch.

**Substitution Yarns**

A: 2 balls Mission Falls *1824 Cotton* 85yds (78m) / 50g (100% cotton) Color: 207

B: 2 balls Mission Falls *1824 Cotton* 85yds (78m) / 50g (100% cotton) Color: 200

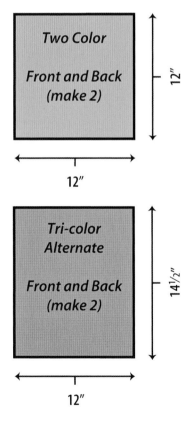

## Shell Sack Pattern

**Front and Back** (make 2)
With A, ch 32.

Row 1: Skip 4 chs, 3 tr in next ch, * skip 2 ch, sc in next ch, skip 2 ch, 7 tr in next ch, repeat from *, ending skip 2 ch, sc in last ch, change to B, turn. (4½ shells)

Row 2: Ch 4, 3 tr in 1st sc, * skip 3 tr, sc in next tr (the center tr of 7-tr group). Skip 3 tr, 7 tr in next sc, repeat from * across ending with sc in top ch of ch-4. Turn. (4½ shells)

Row 3: Ch 4, 3 tr in 1st sc, * skip 3 tr, sc in next tr, skip 3 tr, work 7 tr in next sc, repeat from * across ending with sc in top ch of ch-4. Change to A. (4½ shells)

Rows 4–11: Repeat Rows 2 and 3, 4 more times, following the color patt.

Row 12: Repeat Row 2, 1 more time. Fasten off. Weave in all ends.

**Finishing**
Put 2 pieces tog. Sew the sides and bottom tog with yarn B and yarn needle. Leaving 3" (7.5cm) from seam on either end, sew handles on 1 piece with yarns A and B held tog. Repeat for other piece. Weave in all ends.

**One-Piece Folded Lining** *(see purse lining basics p. 26)*
Measure the width and height of the finished purse. Cut fabric the actual width + ½" (1.25cm) for seam allowance, and twice the height + 3" (7.5cm) for top seam and fold. If your purse is the same size as given finished measurements, trim should measure:

12" (30.5cm) wide + ½" (1.25cm) = 12½" (31.75cm) wide

[12" (30.5cm) high x 2] + 3" (7.5cm) = 27" (68.5cm) high

For the lining, fold in half lengthwise (RS) tog to: 12½" (31.75cm) wide x 13½" (34.25cm) high. Sew tog along side seams leaving ¼" (6mm) seam allowance. Fold top edge over ¾" (2cm) on (WS) front and (WS) back and iron. Pin the lining to the inside of the bag and hand stitch the top edge using a blind stitch.

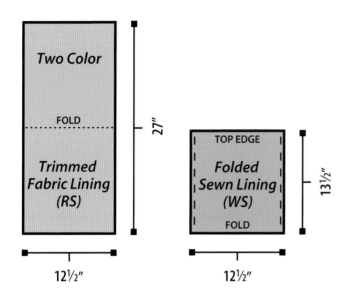

**Two Color**

FOLD

**Trimmed Fabric Lining (RS)**

27"

12½"

TOP EDGE

**Folded Sewn Lining (WS)**

FOLD

13½"

12½"

## Shell Sack Tri-color Alternate Pattern

**Front and Back** (make 2)

Following the color patt:

* 1 row A, 1 row B, 1 row C. Repeat from * 5 more times.

With A, ch 32. Turn.

Rows 1–3: Repeat directions for 2-color Shell Sack.

Rows 4–17: Repeat Rows 2 and 3, 7 more times.

Row 18: Repeat Row 2, 1 more time.

Fasten off. Weave in all ends.

**Finishing**

Put 2 pieces tog. Sew the sides and bottom tog with yarn C and yarn needle. Leaving 3" (7.5cm) from seam on either end, sew handles on 1 piece with yarns A, B, and C held tog. Repeat for other piece. Weave in all ends.

**One-Piece Folded Lining** *(see purse lining basics p. 26)*
Measure the width and height of the finished purse. Cut fabric the actual width + ½" (1.25cm) for seam allowance, and twice the height + 3" (7.5cm) for top seam and fold. If your purse is the same size as given finished measurements, trim should measure:

12" (30.5cm) wide + ½" (1.25cm) = 12½" (31.75cm) wide

[14½" (36.75cm) high x 2] + 3" (7.5cm) = 32" (81.25cm) high

For the lining, fold in half lengthwise (RS) tog to: 12½" (31.75cm) wide x 16" (40.75cm) high. Sew tog along the side seams leaving ¼" (6mm) seam allowance. Fold top edge over ¾" (2cm) on (WS) front and (WS) back and iron. Pin the lining to the inside of the bag and hand stitch the top edge using a blind stitch.

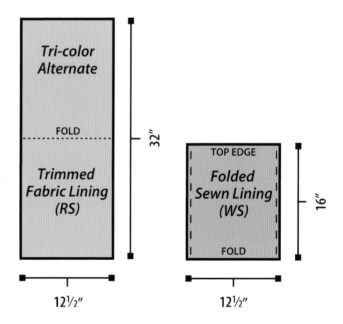

**Tri-color Alternate**

FOLD

**Trimmed Fabric Lining (RS)**

32"

12½"

TOP EDGE

**Folded Sewn Lining (WS)**

FOLD

16"

12½"

# Satchel

*The Satchel's V-shaped pattern uses a long double crochet stitch to accent the fun shape. Super soft alpaca and extra fine merino wool combine to make a beautifully designed purse that is sturdy yet lightweight. The full-length shoulder strap, plush paisley lining, and magnetic snap complete the casual look.*

HANDLES *Crochet*

FABRIC LINING *Cotton*

EMBELLISH *D Rings*

### Yarns

A: 3 balls Plymouth Yarn Company *Suri Merino* 110yds (100m) / 50g (55% suri alpaca, 45% extra fine merino) Color: 207

B: 2 balls Plymouth Yarn Company *Suri Merino* 110yds (100m) / 50g (55% suri alpaca, 45% extra fine merino) Color: 1837

### Crochet Hook

US K/10½ (6.5mm) crochet hook, or size needed to obtain gauge.

### Finishing Materials

2 – 1¾" (4.5cm) D rings

1 – ¾" (2cm) Magnetic snap

1 – Stitch marker

Yarn needle

Lining: cotton fabric 14" (35.5cm) wide x 23" (58.5cm) high

Pocket lining: cotton fabric 6½" (16.5cm) wide x 4¾" (14cm) high

### Finished Measurements

13½" (34.25cm) wide x 11" (28cm) high

### Gauge

15 sts and 20 rows = 4" (10cm) in sc.

### Substitution Yarns

A: 3 balls Reynolds *Andean Alpaca* 110yds (100m) / 50g (100% alpaca) Color: 23

B: 2 balls Reynolds *Andean Alpaca* 110yds (100m) / 50g (100% alpaca) Color: 363

## STITCHES USED

*Slip Stitch (sl)*

*Single Crochet (sc)*

*Single Crochet 3 Together (sc3tog)*

### SPECIAL STITCH

*Long double crochet (ldc)*

Work your dc in st indicated, 3 rnds below the rnd you are currently working. Yo and pull up a loop to the height of the working row. Yo and pull through 2 loops, 2 times.

*V stitch*

Skip st behind ldc, sc in next st, ldc in same st as last ldc (V st made).

# Satchel Pattern

**Front or Back**

With A, ch 49.

Rnd 1: Sc in 2nd ch from hook and in each ch across to end. Turn the ch upside down, so that the sc just worked are on the bottom. Working in unused lps of foundation chain, sc in each ch across. Join with a sl st to 1st sc of rnd. (96 sc)

Rnd 2: Ch 1, sc in 1st sc and in each sc around. Join with a sl st to 1st sc of rnd.

Rnd 3: Repeat Rnd 2. Change to B.

Rnd 4: Ch 1, sc in 1st sc. * Ldc in next st 3 rows below foundation chain, skip st behind ldc, sc in next st, ldc in same st as last ldc (V st made), skip st behind ldc, sc in next st. Repeat from * around. Join with a sl st to 1st sc of rnd. Change to A. (24 V sts)

Rnds 5–7: Repeat Rnd 2, 3 times. Change to B.

Rnd 8: Ch 1, sc in each of the next 2 sts. * Ldc in next st 3 rows below [between 1st and 2nd V sts of last V st row], skip st behind ldc, sc in next st, ldc in same st as last ldc (V st made), sc in next st. Repeat from * around to last 2 sts. Sc in each of last 2 sts. Join with sl st to 1st sc of rnd. Change to A. (23 V sts)

Rnds 9–11: Repeat Rnd 2, 3 times. Change to B.

Rnd 12: Ch 1, sc in 1st sc. * Ldc in next st 3 rows below (before 1st V st of last V st row). Skip st behind ldc, sc in next st, ldc in same st as last ldc. (V st made) *. Repeat from * around. Join with sl st to 1st sc of rnd. Change to A. (24 V sts)

Rnds 13–15: Repeat Rnd 2, 3 times. Change to B.

Rnd 16: Repeat Rnd 8. Change to A.

Rnds 17–19: Repeat Rnd 2, 3 times. Change to B.

Rnd 20: Repeat Rnd 12. Change to A.

Rnds 21–44: Repeat Rnds 13–20, 3 more times.

Rnds 45–47: With color A, ch 1, sc in each st around. Join with a sl st to 1st sc. (96 sc)

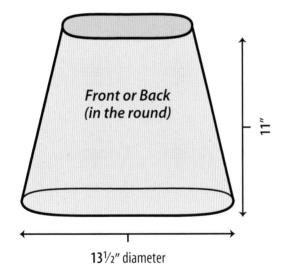

**Front or Back (in the round)**

11"

13½" diameter

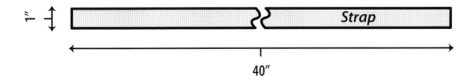

1"

**Strap**

40"

**Rnd 48:** Ch 1, * sc in each of the next 3 sts. Sc3tog over next 3 sts *. Repeat from * to * around. Join with a sl st to 1st st. (64 sts)

**Rnd 49:** Repeat Rnd 48, ending with sc in last 4 sts. (44 sts)

**Rnds 50–55:** Ch 1, * sc in each of the next 7 sts. Sc3tog over next 3 sts . Repeat from * around to last 4 sts. Sc in each of the last 4 sts. Join with a sl st to 1st sc. (36 sts)

### Strap

With A, ch 150.

**Row 1:** Sc in 2nd ch from hook and in each ch across. Turn.

**Rows 2–5:** Ch 1, work 1 sc in each sc across. Turn.

At the end of Row 5, fasten off.

### Finishing

With yarn and yarn needle, sew D rings to the top corners of the bag. With yarn and yarn needle sew each strap end to D rings. Weave in all ends.

### One-Piece Folded Lining *(see purse lining basics p. 26)*

Measure width and height of finished purse. Cut fabric the actual width + ½" (1.25cm) for seam allowance, and twice the height + 1" (2.5cm) for top seam and fold. If your purse is the same size as given finished measurements, trim should measure:

13½" (34.25cm) wide + ½" (1.25cm) = 14" (35.5cm) wide

[11" (28cm) high x 2] + 1" (2.5cm) = 23" (58.5cm) high

For the pocket, cut fabric 6½" (16.5cm) wide x 4¾" (12cm) high. For the side and bottom edges, with (WS) facing, fold over ¼" (6mm) and iron. For top edge, with (WS) facing, fold over ¼" (6mm) and iron. Then, fold over ¼" (6mm) and iron again. Hand stitch the top edge with a blind stitch. With the (RS) facing, pin the pocket to the lining. Position the top of the pocket 1" (2.5cm) from the top edge of the lining and center the pocket from the sides. Hand stitch the side and bottom edges using a blind stitch.

For the lining, fold in half lengthwise (RS) tog to: 14" (35.5cm) wide x 11½" (29.25cm) high. Place 2 pins centered along the top edge 10½" (26.75cm) apart. Sew tog along side seams from the bottom of each corner of the fold to the top edge pins, leaving ¼" (6mm) seam allowance. Fold top edge over ½" (1.25cm) on (WS) front and (WS) back and iron. Trim extra fabric. See page 29 for attaching the magnetic snap. Pin the lining to the inside of the bag and hand stitch the top edge using a blind stitch.

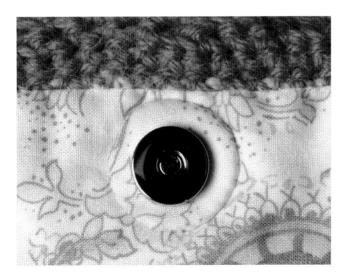

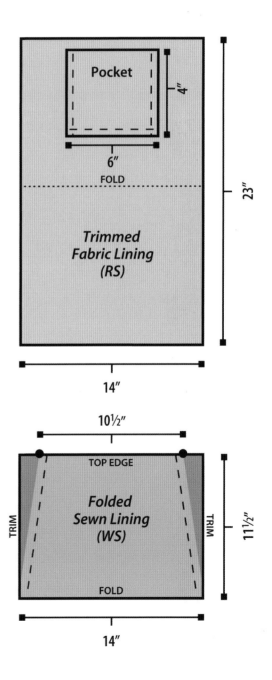

# Beaded Evening Purse

*Designed to carry only the basics, the stunning Beaded Evening Purse features both a single and double crochet stitch pattern. A mix of silky soft alpaca, merino, and silk yarns make this sassy little bag a big hit for that special occasion. The ruffled collar and ruby red beads give this fashion accessory plenty of pop.*

HANDLES *Crochet*

FABRIC LINING *Faux Suede*

EMBELLISH *Red E Beads*

**Yarn**

1 ball Jo Sharp Alpaca *Silk Georgette* 142yds (130m) / 50g (40% alpaca, 40% merino, 20% silk) Color: 751 Pebble

**Crochet Hook**

US F/5 (3.75mm) crochet hook, or size needed to obtain gauge.

**Finishing Materials**

1140 – Red E beads

Lining: faux suede fabric 5" (12.75cm) wide x 14" (35.5cm) high

**Finished Measurements**

4½" (11.5cm) wide x 6½" (16.5cm) high

**Gauge**

24 sts and 16 rows = 4" (10cm) in 1 dc and 1 sc row beaded patt.

**Substitution Yarn**

2 balls Lang Yarns *Fantomas* 160yds (146m) / 50g (75% wool, 18% nylon, 7% acrylic) Color: 0003

## STITCHES USED

*Slip Stitch (sl st)*

*Single Crochet (sc)*

*Double Crochet (dc)*

### SPECIAL STITCHES

*Beaded Chain*

Slip the bead close to the hook, yo, pull through the lp on the hook.

*Beaded Double Crochet (bdc)*

Slip the bead close to the hook. Yo, insert the hook into the st indicated. Yo, pull through the st, yo, and pull through 2 lps. Yo, and pull through the last lps. Bead will be on the (RS).

*Beaded Single Crochet (bsc)*

Slip the bead close to the hook, insert the hook into the st indicated, yo and pull through the st. Yo, and pull through 2 lps. Push the beads through to the (RS).

*Scallop*

(dc, ch 1, dc, ch 1, dc, ch 1, dc) in sp indicated.

*Beaded Scallop*

1 dc, beaded ch 1, 1 dc, ch 1, 1 dc, beaded ch 1, 1 dc in sp indicated.

# Beaded Evening Purse Pattern

**Front and Back** (make 2)

**Folded Ruffle**

String all beads before starting.

With Alpaca Silk Georgette, ch 54.

Row 1: (WS) Work 1 beaded scallop in 6th ch from hook. * Skip 3 ch, work 1 beaded scallop in next ch. Repeat from * across. Turn. (13 beaded scallops)

Row 2: (RS) Ch 3 (counts as 1st dc here and throughout), * work 1 scallop in middle ch-1 sp of beaded scallop in row below. Repeat from * ending with 1 dc in 5th ch of ch-5. Turn. (13 scallops)

Row 3: Ch 3, *. In center ch-1 sp of next scallop work 1 beaded scallop. Repeat from * across, ending with 1 dc in top ch of ch-3. Turn. (13 beaded scallops)

Row 4: Ch 3, * center ch-1 sp of next beaded scallop, work 1 scallop. Repeat from * to last section. Work 1 dc in last ch-1 sp. Turn. (13 scallops)

Fasten off.

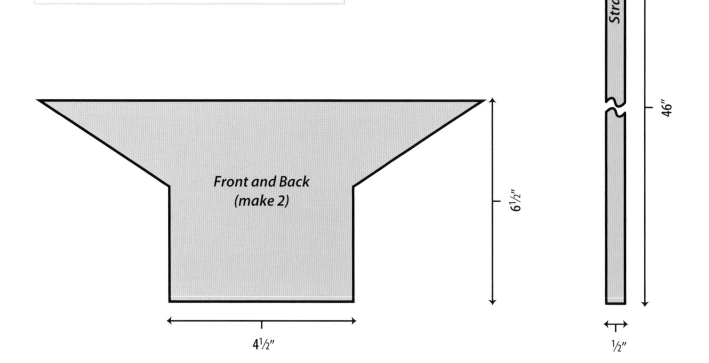

**Front and Back (make 2)**

4½"

6½"

**Strap**

46"

½"

## Body of Bag

Working in single strand of foundation ch of ruffle with (WS) facing, sl st in corner.

Row 1: Sc in 1st ch, * sc in ch-3 sp, sc in next st. Repeat from * ending with 1 sc in last ch of beg ch-3. Turn. (27 sc)

Row 2: Ch 3, skip 1st sc, dc in back lp only of next sc and in every sc across. Turn. (27 dc)

Rows 3–5: Ch 3, skip 1st dc, dc in every st across. Turn.

Row 6: Ch 3, skip 1st dc. Beaded dc in each dc across. Dc in last st. Turn.

Row 7: Ch 1, beaded sc in every st across row, ending with 1 sc in top of ch-3. Turn.

Rows 8–25: Repeat Rows 6 and 7, 9 times.

Fasten off.

## Strap

Ch 4.

Row 1: Sc in 2nd ch from hook and each ch across. Turn. (3 sc)

Row 2: Ch 1, sc in each ch across. Turn. (3 sc)

Repeat Row 2 for approx 46" (116.75cm).

## Finishing

Sew the front and back pieces of the bag tog. After the bag is lined, beginning 2" (5cm) from the top edges, sew strap to inside side seams on both sides.

**One-Piece Folded Lining** (*see purse lining basics p. 26*)
Measure the width and the height of the finished purse. Cut fabric the actual width + ½" (1.25cm) for side seam allowance, and twice the height plus 1" (1.25cm) for the top seam and fold. If your purse is the same size as the given finished measurements, trim should measure:

4½" (11.5cm) wide + ½" (1.25cm) = 5" (12.75cm) wide

[6½" (16.5cm) high x 2] + 1" (2.5cm) = 14" (35.5cm) high

Fold in half lengthwise (RS) tog to: 5" (12.75cm) wide x 7" (17.75cm) high. Sew tog along the side seams leaving a ¼" (6mm) seam allowance. Fold top edge over ½" (1.25cm) on (WS) front and (WS) back and iron. Pin the lining to the inside of the bag and hand stitch the top edge using a blind stitch.

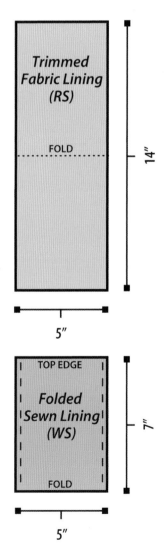

# Harlequin Barrel Bag

*The barrel shaped bag features a unique harlequin crisscross overlay design. Natural variegated wool gives the purse a gradual striping that's both stylish and attractive. The circular sides are worked in the round. Finish it off with an overlay technique that surrounds the bag in a smart diamond pattern. Accent with six gold dome buttons and you're ready for any occasion.*

HANDLES *Crochet*

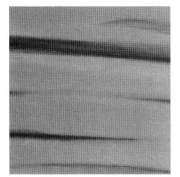

FABRIC LINING *Corduroy*

EMBELLISH *Gold Round Buttons*

## Yarns

A: 4 skeins Knit One, Crochet Too *Paint Box* 100yds (91m) / 50g (100% wool) Color: 02 Adobe Rose

B: 1 skein Knit One, Crochet Too *18 Karat* 224yds (205m) / 25g (65% viscose, 35% metalized polyester) Color: 320 Peach Gold

## Crochet Hooks

US H/8 (5mm) and US D/3 (3.25mm) crochet hooks, or sizes needed to obtain gauge.

## Finishing Materials

2 – 2" (5cm) Gold rings

14 – Safety pin stitch markers

6 – Gold round buttons

2 – 6½" (16.5cm) Plastic needlepoint canvas circles

12¼" (31.25cm) x 18½" (47cm) Plastic needlepoint canvas

Ruler

Lining: corduroy fabric – 4 Side circles 7½" (19cm) diameter

Lining: corduroy fabric – 2 Body pieces 13½" (34.25cm) wide x 22½" (57.25cm) high

## Finished Measurements

13" (33cm) wide x 7" (17.75cm) high x 7" (17.75cm) deep

## Gauge

12 sts and 7 rows = 4" (10cm) in dc.

## Substitution Yarns

A: 4 skeins Noro *Silk Garden* 109yds (100m) / 50g (45% silk, 45% kid mohair, 10% lambs wool) Color: 084

B: 1 skein Trendsetter Yarns *Jester* 110yds (100m) / 25g (80% Viscose, 20% polyamide) Color: 10 Pink Gold

# Harlequin Barrel Bag Pattern

**Front or Back**
With A, ch 41.

Row 1: Bullion st in 4th ch from hook, dc in next ch, * bullion st in next ch, dc in next ch. Repeat from * across. Turn. (39 sts: 19 bullions, 20 dc, including the 1st ch-3)

Row 2: Ch 3 (counts as dc here and throughout), skip 1st dc, dc in each st across. (39 dc)

Rows 3–34: Repeat row 2, 32 times.

Row 35: Ch 3, skip 1st dc, * bullion st in next dc, dc in next dc. Repeat from * across. Fasten off.

**Circular Sides** (make 2)
*Note: You will be working in rnds.*
With A, ch 4. Join with sl st in 1st ch to form a ring.

Rnd 1: Ch 3 (counts as 1 dc here and throughout), work 7 dc in ring. Join with a sl st in 3rd ch of beg ch-3. (8 dc)

Rnd 2: Ch 3, dc in same st as joining. 2 dc in each dc around. Join with a sl st in 3rd ch of beg ch-3. (16 dc)

Rnd 3: Ch 3, dc in same st as joining. 2 dc in each st around. Join with a sl st in 3rd ch of beg ch-3. (32 dc)

Rnd 4: Ch 3, dc in same st as joining. * Dc in each of the next 2 sts. 2 dc in next st. Repeat from * to last 2 sts. Dc in each of the last 2 sts. Join with a sl st in 3rd ch of beg ch-3. (42 dc)

Rnd 5: Ch 3, dc in same st as joining. * Dc in next st, 2 dc in next st. Repeat from * around. Join with a sl st in 3rd ch of beg ch-3. (63 dc)

Rnd 6: Ch 3, skip 1st dc, * bullion st in next st, dc in next st. Repeat from * around to end. Bullion st in same st as beg ch-3. Join with sl st in 3rd ch of beg ch-3. (63 sts)

Fasten off. Weave in loose ends.

**Strap**
With A, ch 11.

Row 1: Dc in 4th ch from hook, and in each ch across. Turn. (9 dc)

Row 2: Ch 3, skip 1st dc, dc in each st across. Turn. (9 dc)

Rows 3–34: Repeat Row 2, 32 more times.

Fasten off. Weave in loose ends.

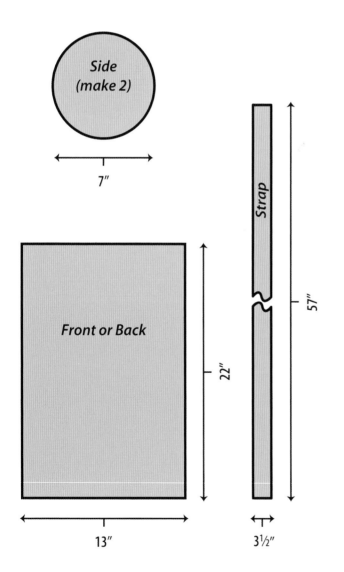

Side (make 2)

7"

Strap

57"

Front or Back

22"

13"

3½"

## Harlequin Overlay

### Spacing and Marking

On (RS) starting from the left top edge, measure 1" (2.5cm) to the right, PM. Measure 2" (5cm) to the right of this marker, PM. Continue to measure 2" (5cm), placing a marker at these points, to the end.

### Stitching the Overlay

With B and D/3 hook, beginning with 1st marker, lay ruler on a diagonal. PM at both ends of ruler. Using the overlay st, follow this diagonal line. Place 2nd marker to the right of the 1st marker. Make sure there are 2" (5cm) between each marker. Continue with each marker across the top and bottom edge of the diagonal line. Do not remove markers until all overlay sts are complete. Secure the ends on the (WS).

### Cross Lines

Work cross lines as you worked the 1st overlay sts, but shift the diagonal the opposite way to form a diamond harlequin patt. Tie all ends securely on (WS).

### Finishing

With (RS) tog and using A, whipstitch side circles to the rectangle on side edges. Leave a 1" (2.5cm) opening at the top.

On (RS), using safety pin stitch markers, pin gold ring to the top of the 5th row of each side circle. Sew gold rings to outside of circular sides with B. Sew the ends of the strap to the gold rings with B.

Sew 3 gold buttons to the top edge of the bag and repeat for other side. Slide clear elastic bands over buttons to close the bag.

### Cylinder Lining *(see purse lining basics p. 28)*

For the lining, you will sew fabric sleeve linings for the plastic supports, then insert into the finished bag. Measure the side diameter height and width of the finished purse. For side circles, cut four circles, the actual diameter of the side circles of the purse + ½" (1.25cm) for seam allowance. For the fabric body width, cut fabric the width of the purse + ½" (1.25cm) for side seam allowance. For the fabric body height, cut fabric the diameter of the side circle x 3.14 (Pi) + ½" (1.25cm) for side seam allowance.

If your purse is the same size as the given finished measurements, trim should measure:

### Side Circles (make 4)

7" (17.75cm) diameter + ½" (1.25cm) = 7½" (19cm) diameter

### Body (make 2)

Fabric width: 13" (33cm) + ½" (1.25cm) = 13½" (34.25cm)

Fabric height: [7" (17.75cm) diameter x 3.14] = 21.98" [rounded to 22" (56cm)] + ½" (1.25cm) = 22½" (57.25cm)

For the body lining, place 2 (RS) fabrics tog. Sew bottom and side seams tog leaving a ¼" (6mm) seam allowance. Turn right side out and insert plastic canvas. Fold excess fabric to inside and hand stitch seam closed.

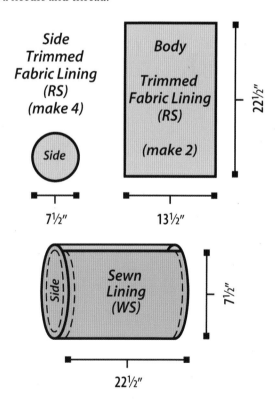

For the lining of the side circles, place 2 (RS) fabrics tog. Sew seams tog, leaving a ¼" (6mm) seam allowance with a 4" (10cm) opening. Turn right side out and insert plastic circle canvas. Fold excess fabric to inside and hand stitch seam closed. Repeat for other side.

Place side circle lining on a flat surface. With short side, wrap lining body around circumference of side circle and pin in place. Repeat for the other side. With needle and matching thread, sew lined pieces tog to form barrel shape. Insert canvas in the bag. Sew lining to the top edges of bag with a needle and thread.

Side Trimmed Fabric Lining (RS) (make 4)

Side

7½"

Body Trimmed Fabric Lining (RS) (make 2)

22½"

13½"

Side

Sewn Lining (WS)

7½"

22½"

# Messenger Bag

*Worn across the body, the sturdy wool, mohair, and acrylic blend of the Messenger Bag features a Tunisian knit stitch, which resembles a basic knit pattern. The circular strap and oversized ivory buckle make this bag a trendy design original. Great for the fall or winter season, it's the perfect accessory for any outfit.*

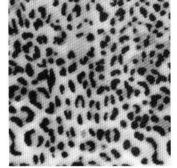

HANDLES *Crochet*

FABRIC LINING *Corduroy*

EMBELLISH *Buckle*

**Yarn**
5 balls Plymouth *Yukon Print* 59yds (54m) / 100g (35% mohair, 35% wool, 30% acrylic) Color: 8004

**Crochet Hook**
US P (10mm) Tunisian crochet hook, or size needed to obtain gauge.

**Finishing Materials**
8 – 2" (5cm) metal craft rings

1 – Buckle with 2" (5cm) slot (MJ Trim)

1 – ¾" (2cm) Magnetic snap

Yarn needle

Stitch marker

Lining: corduroy fabric 15½" (40cm) wide x 20" (50.75cm) high

Pocket lining: corduroy fabric 6½" (16.5cm) wide x 8¾" (22.25cm) high

**Finished Measurements**
15" (38cm) wide x 9½" (24cm) high

**Gauge**
8 sts and 12 rows = 4" (10cm) in Tunisian knit stitch.

**Substitution Yarn**
8 balls Lana Grossa *Caldo Print* 38yds (34.75m) / 50g (100% wool) Color: 20

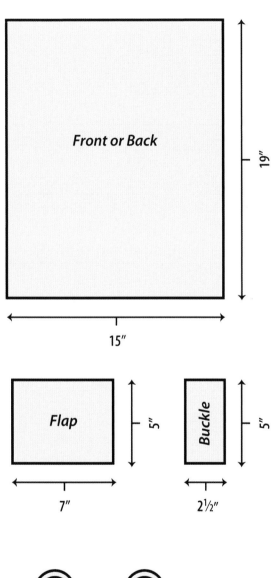

**Front or Back**

15"

19"

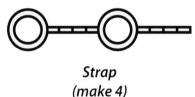

**Flap**

7"

5"

**Buckle**

2½"

5"

**Strap**
**(make 4)**

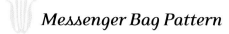

## Messenger Bag Pattern

### Front or Back
*Tunisian Knit Stitch (Tks)*
Ch 30.

Row 1 (forward row): Insert hook in 2nd ch from hook, yo, pull lp through ch (leave all lps on hook). * Insert hook into next ch, yo, pull lp through ch. Repeat from * across to end. (30 lps on hook) DO NOT TURN. Return row: Yo, pull through 1st lp. * Yo, pull through 2 lps. Repeat from * until 1 lp remains. DO NOT TURN.

*Note: Lp on hook is considered 1st st of next row.*

Row 2 (forward row): Skip 1st st. * Insert hook from front to back through next st, below chains formed by previous return row, and between vertical strands of st, yo, pull through st (leave all lps on hook). Repeat from * across, working under 2 lps on the last st, to form a more firm edge (30 lps on hook). Return row: Yo, pull through 1st lp. * Yo, pull through 2 lps *. Repeat from * until 1 lp remains.

Rows 3–56: Repeat row 2. Fasten off.

### Assembly
Fold piece in half (WS) tog. Sew both sides and bottom, leaving top open.

### Flap
With (RS) facing, PM between 15th and 16th sts. Count 8 sts to the right, PM. Count 8 sts to the left, PM. Join yarn at 1st marked st on the right.

*Tunisian Simple Stitch (Tss)*
Row 1 (forward row): Skip 1st st. * Insert hook from right to left under next single vertical lp, yo and pull through lp (leave all lps on hook). Repeat from * to last marker (16 lps on hook). Return row: Yo, pull through 1st lp. * Yo, pull through 2 lps. Repeat from * until 1 lp remains.

Rows 2–8: Repeat row 1. Fasten off.

### Buckle Strap
*Tunisian Simple Stitch (Tss)*
With (RS) facing, mark center 5 sts on edge of flap. Join yarn at 1st marked st on right.

Row 1 (forward row): Skip 1st st. * Insert hook from right to left under next single vertical lp. Yo and pull through lp (leave all lps on hook). Repeat from * to last marker. (5 lps

on hook). Return row: Yo, pull through 1st lp. * Yo pull through 2 lps. Repeat from * until 1 lp remains.

Rows 2–9: Repeat Row 1.

Fasten off.

### Long Shoulder Strap (make 4 sets)
With metal craft ring and size P Tunisian hook work 22 sc around ring. Join with sl st to beg. Ch 3. Attach next ring with sl st. Work 22 sc around this ring. Join with sl st.

Fasten off.

### Finishing
Join 1 set to another with Tunisian crochet hook and yarn. Start with 2 sets of double rings. Sl st in 1 ring on opposite side from joining ch, ch 3, join with sl st to next set of rings, on opposite side from joining ch. Fasten off. Repeat for all 4 sets. When completed, you will have an 8-chain shoulder strap. Each ring will have a ch-3 connecting the rings.

Sew shoulder strap on either side of bag.

Weave in all ends.

### One-Piece Folded Lining (see purse lining basics p. 26)
Measure width and height of finished purse. Cut fabric the actual width + ½" (1.25cm) for seam allowance, and twice the height + 1" (2.5cm) for top seam and fold. If your purse is the same size as given finished measurements, trim should measure:

15" (38cm) wide + ½" (1.25cm) = 15½" (40cm) wide

19" (48.25cm) + 1" (2.5cm) = 20" (51cm) high

For the pocket, cut fabric 6½" (16.5cm) wide x 8¾" (22.25cm) high. For the side and bottom edges, with (WS) facing, fold over ¼" (6mm) and iron. For top edge, with (WS) facing, fold over ¼" (6mm) and iron. Then, fold over ¼" (6mm) and iron again. Hand stitch the top edge with a blind stitch. With the (RS) facing, pin the pocket to the lining. Position the top of the pocket 1" (2.5cm) from the top edge of the lining and center the pocket from the sides. Hand stitch the side and bottom edges using a blind stitch.

For the lining, fold lining in half (RS) tog to: 15½" (40cm) wide x 10" (25.5cm) high. Sew tog along side seams leaving ¼" (6mm) seam allowance. Fold top edge over ½" (1.25cm) on (WS) front and (WS) back and iron. Attach magnetic snaps to underside of buckle strap and outside of purse. See page 29 for basic instructions for attaching the magnetic snaps. Pin the lining to the inside of the bag and hand stitch the top edge using a blind stitch.

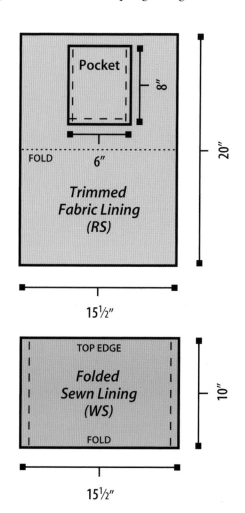

# Resources

*Berroco, Inc.
14 Elmdale Road
P.O. Box 367
Uxbridge, MA 01569
tel: 508.278.2527
www.berroco.com

*Bag-E-Bottoms
437 Maplebrooke Drive East
Westerville, OH 43082
tel: 614.794.9939
www.bag-e-bottoms.com

*Boomerang
Professional Beadlooms & Crochet Hooks
146 Dunham Road
Delhi, NY 13753
tel: 607.746.2107
www.boomerangpro.com

*Crystal Palace Yarns
160 23rd Street
Richmond, CA 94804
tel: 510.237.9988
fax: 510.237.9809
www.straw.com

*Dritz
Prym Consumer USA Inc.
www.dritz.com

*GGH Yarns distributed by:
Muench Yarns
1323 Scott Street
Pentaluma, CA 94954
tel: 707.763.9377
toll free: 800.733.9276
fax: 707.763.9477
www.muenchyarns.com

*Jelly Yarns®
P.O. Box 543
Southampton, PA 18966
tel: 215.953.1415
fax: 215.953.1697
www.jellyyarns.com

Jo Sharp Pty Ltd
P.O. Box 1018
Fremantle 6959
Western Australia
tel: +61.8.9430.9699
fax: +61.8.9430.9499
www.josharp.com.au

Katia distributed by:
Knitting Fever, Inc.
315 Bayview Avenue
Amityville, NY 11701
tel: 516.546.3600
fax: 516.546.6871
www.knittingfever.com

*Knit One, Crochet Too, Inc.
91 Tandberg Trail, Unit 6
Windham, ME 04062
tel: 207.892.9625
fax: 207.892.9903
www.knitonecrochettoo.com

*Louisa Harding Yarns distributed by:
Knitting Fever, Inc. / Euro Yarns
315 Bayview Avenue
Amityville, NY 11701
tel: 516.546.3600
fax: 516.546.6871
www.knittingfever.com

*M&J Trimming
1008 Sixth Avenue
New York, NY 10018
toll free: 1.800.9.MJTRIM
tel: 212.204.9595
www.mjtrim.com

*Muench Yarns
1323 Scott Street
Pentaluma, CA 94954
tel: 707.763.9377
toll free: 800.733.9276
fax: 707.763.9477
www.muenchyarns.com

Nashua Handknits distributed by
Westminster Fibers, Inc.
4 Townsend Avenue, Unit 8
Nashua, NH 03063
tel: 800.445.9276

*Plymouth Yarn Company
500 Lafayette Street
Bristol, PA 19007
tel: 215.788.0459
www.plymouthyarn.com

*Contributors

## About the Author

Carrie A. Sullivan is an accomplished teacher with an affinity for savvy crochet handbag designs. An avid crocheter most of her adult life, she is featuring her original designs in this, her first, book. Carrie's purse patterns are featured in contemporary crocheting and knitting magazines and books including *Knit 1* magazine and *The Knitter's Guide to Combining Yarns*. She lives and works in Southampton, Pennsylvania, with her two sons and husband.

# *Index*

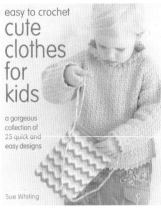

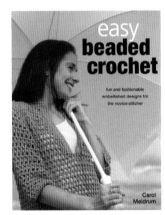